D0940670

FLAVORS OF
AFRICA

FLAVORS OF
AFRICA

DISCOVER AUTHENTIC FAMILY RECIPES FROM ALL OVER THE CONTINENT

EVI AKI FOUNDER OF EV'S EATS

PAGE STREET
PUBLISHING CO.

ST. JOHN THE BAPTIST PARISH LIBRARY
2920 NEW HIGHWAY 51
LAPLACE, LOUISIANA 70068

PAGE STREET
PUBLISHING CO.

Copyright © 2018 Evi Aki

First published in 2018 by

Page Street Publishing Co.

27 Congress Street, Suite 105

Salem, MA 01970

www.pagestreetpublishing.com

All rights reserved. No part of this book may be reproduced or used, in any form or by any means, electronic or mechanical, without prior permission in writing from the publisher.

Distributed by Macmillan, sales in Canada by The Canadian Manda Group.

22 21 20 19 18   1 2 3 4 5

ISBN-13: 978-1-62414-674-9

ISBN-10: 1-62414-674-0

Library of Congress Control Number: 2018943550

Cover and book design by Meg Baskis for Page Street Publishing Co.

Photography by Jakob Layman

Printed and bound in China

Page Street Publishing protects our planet by donating to nonprofits like The Trustees, which focuses on local land conservation.

TO MY MUM, thank you for inspiring me to be brave and for endlessly pouring your love into me, no matter what. You are the reason I love food and being in the kitchen, and for that I am forever grateful.

TO MY FAMILY, I would be nothing without you guys. You make my life rich.

TO MY AUNTY KAINE, my guardian angel. I miss you every day, and you're always in my heart. Thank you for your love and some of the sweetest memories.

CONTENTS

EASTERN
AFRICA 75

NORTHERN
AFRICA 107

SOUTHERN
AFRICA 135

INTRODUCTION

"I ASKED MY MOTHER ONCE, WHERE DOES THE HEART GO
WHEN IT'S RIPPED FROM THE MOTHERLAND? SHE HANDED
ME HER OWN AND SAID, 'WHEREVER YOU CARRY IT'."

—PAVANA REDDY

I grew up in Atlanta, Georgia, as a first-generation Nigerian American. My parents immigrated to the United States in 1990 by way of Austin, Texas, before moving to Chicago, where my two sisters and I were born. Our life in Chicago was filled with a lot of family and, naturally, food. My mum was the second oldest of thirteen children, and she was the "glue" in the family because she took care of all of her younger siblings and naturally fell into a motherhood role. She was also the best cook. Family gatherings and dinner parties were always at our house and were filled with assorted Nigerian and other African dishes, music and laughter. My grandparents would often visit, and I grew up watching my mum and grandmum prepare so many meals. This is where my love affair with food began.

Seven years later we moved away from our extended family to Atlanta, Georgia, which meant fewer family gatherings. But the cooking never stopped. Every Saturday morning my mum would wake up at 6:00 a.m. and head to the farmers' market and African store to get the ingredients she would use to prepare us meals for the upcoming week. When she was back from the store, she would wake the three of us kids up, feed us breakfast and then we'd join her in the kitchen to learn the recipes the way her mum and grandmum taught her. No measurements, no handwritten recipes. Just eyeballing and experience.

I had always told my parents that I wanted to be a doctor, and that was the path I followed in high school and college. It wasn't until I graduated from college and started work as a traveling medical-scribe trainer that I started to remember my love for food. Fast-forward to a year later: I found myself living in Los Angeles. I was new to the city, had very few friends and desperately needed an outlet to express my creativity.

That's how my blog, Ev's Eats, was born. I had started food blogs in the past, but I'd never kept up with them. This time was different. First, I started to cook my way through old family recipes, then I made my way on to new recipes. I wanted to share my recipes because I took pride in making sure they were simple and easy to follow while still being colorful, bold and full of flavor. My blog became a way for me to express myself and make new friends in the food blogging community; but most importantly, it gave me a way to feel close to my family back on the East Coast, my culture and my roots. You see, being from two cultures can be a beautiful thing, but it is hard to balance. At times, I felt I was too American, not proud of my Nigerian heritage. Other times, I felt phony because while my parents were Nigerian, I had never actually lived in Nigeria. I didn't even speak any of their native languages. Cooking helped me identify myself and find my way back to my roots. It gave me confidence as a woman that no matter where I traveled to, no matter how far away I was from my family, as long as I kept my heart with me, I would always have something to be proud of.

This book covers some of my favorite recipes from all over the continent of Africa. Some are from my childhood, foods that I grew up eating. Others I've learned through travel, eating out at restaurants and friends that I've encountered over the years. My goal is to show you that African cooking doesn't have to be intimidating—unlike what the common consensus may be, it's not a cuisine that is hard to prepare. Once you've got the common flavors and ingredients from each region down, the world really is your oyster. See "Stocking Your Pantry for African Cooking" (page 163) for a full list of all the unique ingredients I use in this book. It is my hope that you take the recipes from this book and make them your own. Yes, I want you to follow them, but I also want you to develop your own intuition. If you find you don't like an ingredient, leave it out or substitute it for something you do like. Have fun while cooking your way through this book. Throw on some Afro beats and open your mind to explore a continent full of life, love and delicious food.

Evi Aki

WESTERN AFRICA

The westernmost part of Africa consists of eighteen countries that make up West Africa. This region's cuisine has had a large influence in Western civilizations, due mostly to the centuries-long slave trade, and is commonly known for starchy foods (like rice and yams), leafy vegetables and tropical fruits. I grew up eating West African cuisine, and what I love most about it is the variety of ingredients that taste and feel like they have come directly from the earth. The flavors are exciting and bring a sense of warmth and comfort, as if you're directly nourishing your soul. The recipes in this chapter are broken down into main dishes, side dishes and desserts and beverages.

PARTY JOLLOF RICE

When I was growing up, this popular rice dish made its way onto our dinner table almost every week! It's my favorite rice recipe and is one of the first dishes my mum taught me how to cook. You'll find many versions of this dish, especially as it varies country to country, but the basis is rice that's been spiced and stewed in a flavorful tomato broth. What makes this recipe unique to our family is that we use parboiled white rice, as it can stand up to a long cooking time without getting mushy and soft. I also like to add a dash of curry seasoning to round out the flavors of the tomato. The perfect dinner spread would be rounds of Malta and Guinness, large trays of assorted stewed meat and a huge pan of jollof rice.

MAKES 6 TO 8 SERVINGS

5 medium Roma tomatoes, roughly chopped

1 large red bell pepper, roughly chopped

2 small Scotch bonnet chiles or habanero chiles

¼ cup (60 ml) groundnut oil or vegetable oil

1 medium onion, roughly chopped

3 tbsp (48 g) tomato paste

2½ cups (600 ml) chicken stock

1 tsp salt

½ tsp curry powder

½ tsp dried thyme

1 tsp all-purpose seasoning

1 beef, chicken or vegetable bouillon cube

2 cups parboiled rice, rinsed

3 bay leaves

In a food processor or blender, combine the tomatoes, bell pepper and Scotch bonnet chiles and process for about 45 seconds, making sure everything is blended well. Set the mixture aside, reserving ¼ cup (60 ml) in a small measuring cup.

Heat the oil in a medium pot over medium-high heat. Add the onion and fry just until it turns golden brown, 5 to 7 minutes. Add the tomato paste and fry with the onion for 2 to 3 minutes, stirring occasionally.

Add the blended tomato mixture and cook with the onion and tomato paste for about 30 minutes. Make sure you stir it frequently so that the tomato mixture does not burn.

After 30 minutes, the tomato mixture should have reduced by half and should be a deep red color. Reduce the heat to medium and add the chicken stock. Stir and add the salt, curry powder, thyme, all-purpose seasoning and bouillon cube. Boil for 10 minutes.

Add the rice to the pot, mixing well with the tomato stew. If you need to add water so that the rice is level with the tomato mixture, do so.

Add the bay leaves, cover the pot and cook over medium-low heat for 15 to 30 minutes.

When the liquid has almost entirely evaporated, add the reserved tomato stew, cover and let the mixture cook for 5 to 10 minutes, until the liquid has completely evaporated.

Turn off the heat, mix thoroughly and serve with your choice of assorted meats and fried plantains, if desired.

NIGERIAN RED STEW

Every Nigerian has a pot of this tomato-based stew in their refrigerator right now, I can guarantee you. It's the most iconic dish of Nigeria and is eaten with a lot of our staple foods, like rice, beans, plantains, yams and many other starchy ingredients. The base of this stew is tomato, the same base as Party Jollof Rice (page 13). The stew can be made with fish, chicken, beef or any type of meat or seafood you prefer. My mum made a huge pot of this stew every Saturday, and it would last our family almost an entire week. Her version was made with both beef and chicken. My taste has changed as I've gotten older, so I prefer to make this with chicken alone. My favorite way to enjoy this stew is over parboiled white rice with a boiled egg. I could eat it every day!

MAKES 8 TO 10 SERVINGS

CHICKEN

3 lb (1.4 kg) chicken (any cut)

1 tbsp (3 g) dried thyme

1 tsp garlic powder

1 chicken bouillon cube

Salt and black pepper, as needed

STEW

1½ cups (360 ml) vegetable oil, divided

4 medium Roma tomatoes, roughly chopped

1 (28-oz [784-g]) can whole peeled plum tomatoes, drained

1 large red bell pepper, roughly chopped

2 small habanero chiles

1 medium onion, thinly sliced

2 tbsp (32 g) tomato paste

1 cup (240 ml) chicken stock

1½ tsp (2 g) dried thyme

1 tbsp (8 g) Nigerian red pepper or cayenne pepper

1 tsp all-purpose seasoning

1 chicken bouillon cube

1 bay leaf

To make the chicken, rinse it and cut it into bite-size cubes. Fill a large pot half full of water. Add the chicken cubes, thyme, garlic powder, bouillon cube and salt and black pepper. Bring the water to a boil over high heat, reduce the heat to medium and cook the chicken 15 to 20 minutes, or until its internal temperature is 165°F (74°F).

While the chicken is cooking, preheat the oven to 350°F (177°C).

Remove the chicken from the stock and set aside. To make the stew, heat 1 cup (240 ml) of the oil in a large skillet over medium-high heat. Add the chicken and fry it until it's golden brown on all sides, 5 to 7 minutes. Place the chicken on a large baking sheet and bake for 10 minutes. Set aside.

In a blender, combine the Roma tomatoes, plum tomatoes, bell pepper and habaneros. Blend until the ingredients are pureed.

Heat the remaining ½ cup (120 ml) of oil in a large pot over high heat. Add the onion and cook just until it turns golden brown, about 5 minutes.

Add the tomato puree and cook for about 25 minutes, or until the mixture reduces by half and turns a deep red and the oil begins to separate from the tomatoes. Stir frequently to prevent burning the bottom. Add the tomato paste and cook for 5 minutes. Add the chicken to the pot and stir to combine.

Add the chicken stock, thyme, Nigerian red pepper, all-purpose seasoning, bouillon cube and bay leaf.

Stir the ingredients together and add water if needed. Simmer for 15 minutes.

Serve the stew with rice, beans or any other dish of your choice.

MAAFE

(WEST AFRICAN PEANUT SOUP)

There's something about peanut butter that instantly transports me to childhood. Whether it's a peanut butter sandwich or peanut butter cookies, it's a flavor I can't get enough of. I used to be that child sneaking into the kitchen at night just for a spoonful. This peanut soup is my ode to peanut butter. It's savory, a little spicy and the peanut butter brings a smooth, creamy and nutty finish to the soup.

MAKES 6 TO 8 SERVINGS

1½ lb (680 g) chicken breasts, cut into 2-inch (6-cm) pieces

1 tbsp (15 g) salt, plus more to taste

1 tsp black pepper, plus more to taste

1 small onion, thickly sliced

3 cups (720 ml) water

¼ cup (60 ml) vegetable oil

2 medium tomatoes, roughly chopped

1 medium onion, roughly chopped, divided

3 to 4 cloves garlic, whole

2 to 3 tbsp (6 to 9 g) dried parsley

1 tsp smoked paprika

1 tbsp (8 g) cayenne pepper

½ tsp white pepper

¾ lb (340 g) russet potatoes, roughly chopped

¼ lb (113 g) carrots, roughly chopped

½ cup (90 g) smooth peanut butter

1 small habanero chile, diced

In a large saucepan over high heat, season the chicken with the salt and black pepper. Add the sliced onion and water and boil until the chicken is tender and its internal temperature is 165°F (74°C), about 30 minutes. Remove the chicken, then strain the stock through a sieve and set aside. You should be left with 3 to 4 cups (720 to 960 ml) of stock.

Heat the oil in a large pot over medium heat. Add the chicken and sauté, stirring, just until the pieces begin to brown, 5 to 7 minutes. Remove the chicken from the pot and set it aside. (Keep the pot over the heat.)

While the chicken is browning, combine the tomatoes, half of the chopped onion, garlic and parsley in a blender. Blend the ingredients until they are completely smooth.

Add the remaining half of the chopped onion to the pot and cook for 2 minutes. Pour the blended tomato mixture into the pot. Add the smoked paprika, cayenne and white pepper and stir to combine. Cook for 10 minutes.

Add the potatoes, carrots, peanut butter, habanero and 3 cups (720 ml) of the homemade stock to the pot. Stir the ingredients together and continue to cook until the potatoes are tender, 10 to 15 minutes. Add the chicken and simmer for 5 to 7 minutes. Season with salt and black pepper. Serve with rice.

EGUSI SOUP

I have a love-hate relationship with egusi soup. Love, because the taste of egusi is like no other. It's earthy, nutty and tastes like a cross between a ground-up mushroom and nuts. The seeds look like watermelon seeds but taste nothing like them. The hate comes in with the way egusi soup was prepared while I was growing up. Traditionally, a lot of West African soups have an assortment of meat and fish. My mum would make egusi with beef, chicken, tripe and dried fish, and I wasn't a fan of a lot of those ingredients. Now that I can make my own, I use only beef, making it my perfect pot of egusi soup. If you're unfamiliar with egusi, see page 165.

MAKES 6 TO 8 SERVINGS

1½ lb (680 g) beef stew meat

Salt and black pepper, as needed

1 tbsp (3 g) dried thyme

1 small onion, roughly chopped

1 cup (240 ml) water

6 cups (1.4 L) beef stock

4 cups (600 g) egusi melon seeds, ground

1 large onion, roughly chopped

2 small habanero chiles, stems removed

¾ cup (180 ml) palm oil

4 tbsp (85 g) bitter leaf, washed

6 cups (180 g) roughly chopped spinach

3 tbsp (18 g) ground crayfish

1 tbsp (8 g) Nigerian red pepper

Fufu (page 49), for serving

Rinse the beef and pat the pieces completely dry with a paper towel. In a large pot over high heat, combine the beef, salt and black pepper, thyme and onion. Add the water and bring the mixture to a boil.

Cover the pot, reduce the heat to medium and cook for 1 hour, until the meat's internal temperature is 150°F (66°C) and the meat is tender.

Strain the cooking water through a sieve and set the beef aside.

Add the beef stock to a large pot over medium heat. Add the ground egusi to the stock and stir. The consistency should be similar to the thickness of half-and-half.

Cover the pot and cook until the egusi starts to dry or cake, about 25 minutes. Stir and add a little water regularly to make sure the mixture does not burn. It's ready when egusi oil rises to the surface.

In a food processer, blend the large onion and habaneros together to form a sauce.

Add the palm oil, onion-habanero sauce and bitter leaf and cook for 7 to 10 minutes, stirring frequently.

Add the cooked beef and spinach and stir together. Add the ground crayfish, the Nigerian red pepper and the salt to taste. Cover the pot and simmer for 15 minutes.

Turn off the heat and let the soup cool for 5 minutes before serving. Serve with Fufu.

YASSA
(SENEGALESE LEMON CHICKEN)

This chicken is bright in flavor and super tender and moist. The acidity of the lemon really helps break down the chicken. As a result, the meat absorbs all the flavors while melting in your mouth. I love to enjoy this chicken with a bowl of white rice.

MAKES 6 SERVINGS

4 boneless, skinless chicken breasts

4 chicken drumsticks

4 cups (460 g) sliced onions

⅓ cup (80 ml) fresh lemon juice

1 tsp salt

½ tsp black pepper

1 small habanero chile, seeded and minced

1½ tbsp (23 ml) peanut oil

1½ cups (360 g) chicken stock

½ cup (75 g) pimento-stuffed olives

½ cup (120 ml) water

1 tbsp (16 g) Dijon mustard

Rice, for serving

Place the chicken breasts and drumsticks in a large resealable bag. Add the onions, lemon juice, salt, black pepper and habanero to the bag. Seal the bag and massage the chicken with the contents of the bag. Place the bag in the fridge for 3 hours to marinate.

Heat the oil in a large Dutch oven over medium-high heat. Add all of the contents of the bag to the Dutch oven. Cook for 10 minutes, browning the chicken. Add the stock, olives, water and mustard. Bring the mixture to a boil, then reduce the heat to medium-low and simmer, uncovered, for 1 hour.

Serve over rice.

SUYA
(SPICY GRILLED KEBABS)

Meet the epitome of Nigerian street food. Every town has its go-to spot for this delicious, spicy roasted meat, and I have amazing memories of seeing hundreds of these sticks of meat turning on the smoky grill. The smell alone will make you hungry, but then biting into one will instantly awaken your taste buds. Have a glass of ice water ready for this one, because the spice is out of this world!

MAKES 5 TO 6 SERVINGS

Vegetable oil, as needed

¼ cup (43 g) roasted almonds

2 tbsp (16 g) cayenne pepper or Nigerian red pepper

2 tsp (6 g) smoked paprika

1 tbsp (8 g) garlic powder

1 tbsp (8 g) onion powder

1 tbsp (8 g) white pepper

1 chicken bouillon cube

Salt, to taste

2 lb (900 g) sirloin or chuck roast

NOTE: Feel free to use the suya spice mix to season other cuts of meat—it's great on fish and chicken as well!

Soak 8 to 10 wooden skewers in water for at least 20 minutes before cooking to prevent them from burning.

If you will be preparing the kebabs in the oven, preheat the oven to 450°F (232°C). Lightly oil a large baking sheet or roasting pan to prevent the suya from sticking to the pan.

Grind the roasted almonds in a coffee or spice grinder until they are finely ground. Take care to not grind the nuts into a paste.

In a medium bowl, mix the cayenne, paprika, garlic powder, onion powder, white pepper, bouillon cube and salt. Add the ground almonds to the spice mixture and set aside. This is the suya spice mix.

Pat the sirloin dry with a paper towel and slice it diagonally into thin strips.

Thread the sirloin onto the soaked skewers with about 4 to 5 pieces of meat per skewer. Rub oil on the beef so that the spice mixture will adhere to the meat.

Pack the seasoning onto the beef by rubbing the suya spice mix on all sides of the meat. Each piece of meat should be coated evenly with the suya spice mix.

If you will be roasting the kebabs, place the skewers on the baking sheet. Bake for 12 to 15 minutes. After 15 minutes, place the skewers in the broiler and broil for 5 minutes. The meat should reach an internal temperature of 150°F (74°C).

If you will be grilling the kebabs, make sure the grill is extremely hot (almost to the point of smoking). Place the skewers directly on the grill and grill for 10 to 15 minutes, turning occasionally. The meat should reach an internal temperature of 150°F (74°C).

Serve the kebabs with sliced onions and tomatoes.

EWA OLOYIN
(ONE-POT BEANS AND PLANTAIN)

My dad loves beans. He can make a pot of beans like no other. I, on the other hand, have a love-hate relationship with beans. It seems like I've never been able to enjoy them on their own and always need something to accompany them. My solution to that conundrum is this recipe. Some of my favorite ingredients, like palm oil and plantain, are included here—having other ingredients in the pot of beans enhances the flavor and breaks up the monotony of only having beans. I love the texture the spinach and plantains add.

MAKES 6 SERVINGS

2 cups (303 g) dried black-eyed peas, soaked overnight

4 cups (960 ml) water

¾ cup (180 ml) palm oil

3 tbsp (18 g) ground crayfish

1 small habanero chile, finely chopped

1 beef or chicken bouillon cube

1 large ripe plantain, cut into ¼-inch (6-mm) thick rounds

2 cups (60 g) tightly packed spinach, roughly chopped

Salt, to taste

Place the black-eyed peas and water in a large pot and bring them to a boil over medium-high heat.

Using a spoon, remove the layer of foam from the top of the water. Reduce the heat to medium, cover the pot and let the black-eyed peas simmer for 15 minutes.

Add the palm oil, ground crayfish and habanero and continue to simmer for 1 hour, checking frequently. If you find that the liquid is absorbed too quickly, you can add water as needed.

Stir in the bouillon cube and plantain, cover the pot and continue to simmer for 30 minutes.

Stir in the spinach 5 minutes before the black-eyed peas are done, then season with salt.

Serve the beans by themselves or with some rice.

PLANTAIN FRITTATA

This frittata is just like the Spicy Nigerian Omelet (page 37), except instead of sardines, plantains are used. This is a great recipe for a holiday morning when you need to cook eggs for a large crowd and don't want to do so individually. Adding the sliced plantains on top adds a layer of sweetness to the frittata, and the best part is the crunchiness imparted by baking the plantains until they are deliciously crispy.

MAKES 4 TO 5 SERVINGS

2 large ripe plantains

¼ cup (60 ml) vegetable oil, divided

1 medium onion, diced

1 small habanero chile, diced

1 large bell pepper (any color), diced

1 small tomato, diced

1 tsp minced garlic

6 large eggs

¼ cup (10 g) fresh cilantro, roughly chopped

2 tbsp (30 ml) milk

1 tsp paprika

1 tsp dried thyme

Preheat the oven to 350°F (177°C).

Slice the plantains into rounds about ¼ inch (6 mm) thick.

Heat 2 tablespoons (30 ml) of vegetable oil in a large ovenproof skillet over medium-high heat. Add the plantain rounds and fry them for 2 minutes per side, until they are soft and golden. Remove the plantain rounds from the skillet and set aside.

Heat the remaining oil in the skillet and add the onion, habanero, bell pepper, tomato and garlic and sauté for 5 to 10 minutes, stirring frequently. Remove the skillet from the heat.

In a medium bowl, mix together the eggs, cilantro, milk, paprika and thyme. Pour the egg mixture into the skillet.

Carefully place the plantain rounds on top of the egg mixture.

Transfer the skillet to the oven, placing it on the middle rack. Bake for 30 to 40 minutes, until the center of the frittata is firm.

Allow the frittata to cool before serving.

MUM'S CORNED BEEF AND SPINACH STEW

Heading to the African store to restock on the essentials that we couldn't find in regular grocery stores was something we did weekly as I was growing up. Whenever my mum would get a case of yams, I knew this corned beef and spinach stew would be making its way to the dinner table soon. Canned corned beef brings me such nostalgia—it was also a rare treat when I was growing up because of the price. So this dish has always been very special to me. The sweetness and saltiness from the corned beef mixes well with the spinach, making this the perfect stew to serve with some boiled yams and fried plantains.

MAKES 4 TO 6 SERVINGS

2 tbsp (30 ml) vegetable oil

1 medium onion, roughly chopped

1 small habanero chile, minced

1 large Roma tomato, roughly chopped

2 (12-oz [336-g]) cans corned beef

2 lb (900 g) roughly chopped spinach

1 tbsp (8 g) Nigerian red pepper

2 tsp (6 g) garlic powder

1 tsp onion powder

1 chicken bouillon cube

1 tbsp (8 g) all-purpose seasoning

Boiled yams, for serving, optional

Boiled or fried plantains, for serving, optional

Heat the oil in a large skillet over medium-high heat. Add the onion, habanero and tomato and sauté for 10 minutes.

Add the corned beef to the skillet, breaking it up into smaller pieces. Sauté for 5 to 7 minutes, stirring frequently.

Reduce the heat to medium and add the spinach, stirring until it begins to wilt. Add the Nigerian red pepper, garlic powder, onion powder, bouillon cube and all-purpose seasoning and stir to combine.

Cook for 7 to 10 minutes, until all the spinach has wilted.

Serve the stew with boiled yams, fried or boiled plantains or rice.

GRILLED TILAPIA WITH GINGER-PEPPER MARINADE

When I was little, the sight of a whole fish would send me into a panic. It wasn't until I watched my mum clean and prepare the fish with this delicious, vibrant stew that I started to grow interested. As soon as this fish hit the table at dinner parties, everyone would go nuts. My mum would divide it up, and the result was always moist, flaky fish with a deliciously sweet sauce.

MAKES 4 TO 6 SERVINGS

4 whole tilapia, washed and cleaned thoroughly

2 tsp (10 g) salt

2 tsp (6 g) black pepper

2 medium lemons

2 tsp (6 g) ground African nutmeg (ehuru)

2 tsp (5 g) star anise seeds

½ cup fresh cilantro

1 (1-inch [5-cm]) piece fresh ginger, peeled

10 cloves garlic

1 tsp smoked paprika

1 chicken bouillon cube

1 medium onion, roughly chopped

Vegetable oil, as needed

Rice, for serving

Place the tilapia in a large roasting pan. Make 3 diagonal slits on each side of the tilapia. Do not cut through the fish to the other side. Season the fish generously on each side with the salt and black pepper. Squeeze the lemons all over each side of the fish.

Grind the African nutmeg and star anise seeds together in a spice grinder.

Add the cilantro, ginger, garlic, smoked paprika, bouillon cube, onion and African nutmeg mixture to a food processor and blend until completely smooth.

Pour the marinade over the fish, making sure it is coated evenly. Cover the roasting pan with plastic wrap and allow the tilapia to marinate in the refrigerator for 3 to 4 hours.

Preheat the grill to high heat. While the grill is preheating, heat the oil in a small saucepan over medium heat. Wipe down the grill with the hot oil. Place the tilapia on the grill.

Brush the marinade on one side of the fish and cook for 5 minutes. Flip the fish, brush the other side with marinade and cook for 5 minutes. The fish is cooked when it is white and its juices run clear.

Serve the fish with rice.

GOOD-FOR-THE-SOUL NIGERIAN PEPPER SOUP

Just a spoonful of this pepper soup will instantly clear up a cold. Whenever the whole house was falling ill, or it was an especially cold winter day, my mum would make a large pot of this soup. Just the smell alone would bring such warmth into the house. In Nigeria, pepper soup is often given to women after giving birth to help rebuild their strength and speed up their recovery. Whenever I'm feeling down, I make a pot of this soup for that instant pick-me-up.

MAKES 4 TO 6 SERVINGS

1½ lb (680 g) assorted boneless meats (e.g., beef, goat, chicken), cut into bite-size pieces

1 large onion, roughly chopped

1 (½-inch [13-mm]) piece fresh ginger, peeled

2 cloves garlic

3 beef or chicken bouillon cubes

Salt, as needed

6 cups (1.4 L) water

4 small habanero chiles, thinly sliced

1 tbsp (8 g) cayenne pepper

1 tbsp (8 g) white pepper

3 tbsp (24 g) pepper soup spice mix

Yams, plantains or rice, for serving

Wash the meats thoroughly and transfer them to a large pot. (If you are using goat meat, cook this separately from your other meats as it takes longer to cook.)

In a food processor, combine the onion, ginger and garlic and process until the ingredients are smooth. Add the sauce to the meat, along with the bouillon cubes and salt.

Cover the pot with a lid and cook over medium heat for 10 to 15 minutes to sweat the meat.

Add the water and cook until the meats are soft. (The exact cooking time will depend on the meats you are preparing: beef will require about 60 minutes; chicken will require about 45 minutes; goat will require 90 to 120 minutes.)

Add the habanero, cayenne and white pepper to the meat. Stir the ingredients together and cook for 2 minutes.

Add the pepper soup spice mix and season with additional salt. Stir to combine and cook for 5 minutes.

Serve the soup with yams, plantains or rice.

BUCHI'S OKRA SOUP

Whenever I think of okra soup, my middle sister, Orezi, immediately comes to mind. This is her favorite soup, and my mum says that when she was a baby, she would fight you over it. You just couldn't get it in her mouth fast enough. I now affectionately refer to it as Buchi's Okra Soup: Buchi is short for my sister's middle name, Onyebuchi, which means, "Who is greater than God?"

Okra soup can be quite gelatinous in texture, but fear not: This is the consistency you're looking for. To help add texture to the okra, I like to add fresh spinach leaves right at the end.

MAKES 6 SERVINGS

½ lb (225 g) beef stew meat

Salt and black pepper, as needed

1 medium onion, roughly chopped, divided

2 cups (480 ml) water, divided

½ lb (225 g) bone-in chicken breast, cut into bite-size pieces

1 lb (450 g) fresh okra

1 tbsp (6 g) ground crayfish

1 beef or chicken bouillon cube

1 tbsp (8 g) smoked paprika

1 tbsp (8 g) cayenne pepper

3 cups (90 g) tightly packed spinach, roughly chopped

Banku (page 50) or Fufu (page 49), for serving

In a medium pot, combine the beef, salt and black pepper, half of the onion and 1 cup (240 ml) of the water. In another medium pot, combine chicken, salt and black pepper, the remaining onion and the remaining 1 cup (240 ml) of water. Bring each pot to a boil over high heat and cook for 30 minutes.

While the beef and chicken are boiling, wash the okra and cut off the tops and bottoms. Slice the okra into rounds and transfer them to a food processor. Pulse the food processor until the okra is a coarse consistency.

Strain the beef from its cooking liquid. Add the beef to the chicken. Add the ground crayfish, bouillon cube, smoked paprika and cayenne. Stir to combine and cook for 5 minutes.

Add the spinach and additional salt and black pepper. Cook for 5 minutes.

Stir the soup once more and serve with Banku or Fufu.

SPICY NIGERIAN OMELET

When I was growing up, my parents would put sardines in their eggs, and I always thought that was really weird. Sardines used to gross me out, and I never understood why my parents loved them so much. But recently, my aunt made me this omelet for breakfast, and it completely changed the way I wanted to eat eggs in the morning. The sardines were salty and made the omelet taste so rich! Now I, like my parents, love adding sardines to my eggs.

MAKES 2 TO 4 SERVINGS

2 tbsp (30 ml) olive oil

½ tsp dried thyme

1 tsp curry powder

½ tsp cayenne pepper

½ tsp garlic powder

⅛ tsp ground turmeric

⅛ tsp ground cumin

1 small habanero chile, minced

1 medium red or yellow bell pepper, diced

1 small onion, diced

1 (4-oz [112-g]) can smoked sardines in olive oil

¼ cup roughly chopped fresh basil

4 large eggs

Pinch of salt

Heat the oil in a large skillet over medium-high heat. Add the thyme, curry powder, cayenne, garlic powder, turmeric and cumin and cook until it becomes fragrant, 1 to 2 minutes.

Add the habanero, bell pepper, onion, sardines and basil to the skillet and sauté for 5 minutes.

Meanwhile, whisk the eggs and salt together in a small bowl.

Pour the eggs into the skillet and cook the omelet for 2 minutes on each side.

DODO
(FRIED PLANTAINS)

West Africa boasts a wide selection of fried-plantain recipes. From Nigeria to Cameroon to Liberia to the Ivory Coast, you'll find versions called kelewele, alloco and dodo on almost every street corner. Fried plantains are eaten with many of the rice dishes, soups and stews. They add that touch of sweetness that is sometimes needed with heavily spiced food.

Learning to fry plantains is one of my earliest kitchen memories. Both my mum and grandmum would slice the plantain in their hands, somehow managing to never cut themselves. It was always my goal to learn to cut the plantain just like them. Now, whenever I prepare plantains, I always feel my mum and grandmum in the kitchen with me, their watchful eyes cautioning me to be careful with the knife.

MAKES 4 TO 6 SERVINGS

Vegetable oil, as needed

4 to 6 large ripe plantains (see note)

Salt, to taste

Heat the oil to 375°F (191°C) in a large pot.

While the oil is heating, cut off both ends of the plantains with a sharp knife. Make a shallow incision down the long seams of the plantains. This will make them easier to peel. Peel the plantains' skin away from the fruit.

Cut the plantains into diagonal pieces about 1-inch (3-cm) thick. Place the pieces in a medium bowl.

Sprinkle the salt over the plantains, tossing so that each slice is evenly coated.

Once the oil is hot, add the plantain pieces to the oil in batches. Fry for 3 to 5 minutes until they are golden brown, flipping once after 2 minutes.

Remove the plantains from the oil using a slotted spoon and transfer them to a plate lined with paper towels.

Serve immediately.

NOTE: Look for plantains with little black spots, as these mean the plantains are ripe. Avoid plantains that are too soft.

PILI PILI
(HOT PEPPER SAUCE)

I love hot sauce. It's something that I have with almost every meal. There are so many variations of hot sauce, and I've spent a lot of time testing the ones I love best. When it comes down to the nitty-gritty, it's all about the choice of pepper. This sauce uses one of the hottest chiles known to humanity, the African bird's eye chile. Dip your sweet fried plantains in this sauce and you've got the perfect "sweet and heat" snack.

MAKES 4 TO 5 CUPS (960 ML TO 1.5 L)

12 African bird's eye chiles or 12 small habanero chiles

1 small yellow or red bell pepper, roughly chopped

2 cloves garlic, roughly chopped

1 small onion, roughly chopped

1 large tomato, roughly chopped

¼ cup (60 ml) olive oil

Salt, to taste

In a food processor, combine the African bird's eye chiles, bell pepper, garlic, onion and tomato. Pulse the food processor until the ingredients are finely chopped.

Add the oil and salt and puree the mixture until smooth.

Transfer the sauce to a medium saucepan over medium heat and simmer for 30 minutes, stirring occasionally.

Allow the sauce to cool, then transfer it to clean lidded jars.

Pili Pili can be kept in the refrigerator for up to 2 weeks.

PLANTAIN CHIPS

No trip to the African market was complete until we each picked up our own bag of plantain chips. When I was in college, I didn't have a car, so it was hard for me to get plantain chips whenever I had the craving. I turned to making them on my own and found that they taste really good with both green plantains and ripe plantains. I love eating these on their own, and I'll dip them in Pili Pili (page 41) as well. You can store what's left in an airtight container for up to two weeks.

MAKES 6 TO 8 SERVINGS

4 large green or ripe plantains
1 tbsp (8 g) smoked paprika
2 pinches of salt, divided
Vegetable oil, for frying

Using a mandoline or sharp knife, cut the plantains into round slices about ⅛-inch (3-mm) thick. Transfer the plantain slices to a medium bowl.

Season the plantains with the smoked paprika and 1 pinch of salt and toss so that they are evenly coated.

Heat 3 to 4 cups (720 to 960 ml) of vegetable oil to 350°F (177°C) in a large pot. Fry the plantains in batches until they turn golden brown and crisp, 3 to 5 minutes.

Remove the plantain chips with a slotted spoon and transfer them to a large baking sheet lined with paper towels.

Sprinkle the plantain chips with the remaining 1 pinch of salt and serve.

BOULETTES DE POISSON
(SENEGALESE FRIED FISH BALLS)

My mum would make us eat boxed macaroni and cheese with frozen fish sticks quite frequently while I was growing up. When I was a little kid, I actually used to love that meal—that quickly starting changing the older I got, though. I started to hate those frozen fish sticks and would secretly dread the entire meal. I started making my own fish sticks in the form of these Senegalese Fried Fish Balls. They're the perfect way for me to enjoy fish sticks: never frozen and, of course, a spicy tomato sauce to go with them.

MAKES 4 TO 6 SERVINGS

FISH BALLS

1 lb (450 g) frozen cod fillets, thawed

2 tbsp (30 ml) water

1 slice white bread

1 tsp salt

½ tsp black pepper

2 large eggs

4 cloves garlic

1 scallion, finely chopped

1 small jalapeño, finely chopped

2 tbsp (6 g) chopped fresh parsley

½ cup (63 g) all-purpose flour

Vegetable oil, for frying

SAUCE

2 tbsp (30 ml) vegetable oil

2 scallions, minced

2 medium tomatoes, roughly chopped

1 medium red bell pepper, roughly chopped

1 small jalapeño, seeded and roughly chopped

½ cup (120 ml) water

Salt, to taste

Fresh parsley, for garnish

To make the fish balls, squeeze the fillets to get rid of all the liquid.

Roughly chop the fillets and transfer them to a large bowl. Add the water, bread, salt, black pepper, eggs, garlic, scallion, jalapeño and parsley. Mix the ingredients together and let them stand in the refrigerator for 30 minutes.

Place the flour in a shallow dish. Shape the fish mixture into golf ball–size balls. Roll the fish balls in the flour.

Heat 3 to 4 cups (720 to 960 ml) of the oil in a large skillet over medium-high heat. Add the fish balls and fry them, turning frequently until they are golden brown on all sides, about 10 minutes.

While the fish balls are frying, make the sauce. Heat the oil in a medium saucepan over medium-high heat. Add the scallions, tomatoes, bell pepper and jalapeño and sauté for 5 to 7 minutes. Remove the saucepan from the heat and allow the mixture to cool completely. Once the mixture has cooled, transfer it to a food processor and add the water. Process the mixture to form a sauce. Return the sauce to the pan and cook for 5 minutes. Season with salt.

Add the fish balls to the sauce and cook for 10 minutes over low heat.

Garnish the fish balls with the parsley and serve immediately.

TATALE
(PLANTAIN PANCAKES)

Sometimes I get carried away and buy too many plantains, and I don't manage to cook them all before they get too ripe. If you've ever tried frying an overly ripe plantain, it's a disaster. I discovered this Ghanaian plantain recipe after desperately trying to find something to do with my ripe plantains. I hate wasting food, so throwing the plantains out was not an option. Thankfully, this recipe is the answer to that very problem. I could eat a million of these!

MAKES 4 TO 6 SERVINGS

4 large overly ripe plantains, peeled

1 cup (170 g) cornmeal

4 tbsp (60 ml) milk

1 tsp salt

1 tsp garlic powder

1 tsp grated fresh ginger

1 tsp cayenne pepper

2 scallions, roughly chopped

3 tbsp (45 ml) canola oil

In a large bowl, mash the plantains with a potato masher until they have a pureed consistency.

Add the cornmeal, milk, salt, garlic powder, ginger and cayenne to the mashed plantains. Stir in the scallions until the ingredients are fully combined.

Heat the oil in a large skillet over medium heat.

Use a medium ladle to pour the plantain batter into the skillet. Fry each side of the pancakes for about 5 minutes, until golden brown.

Serve immediately.

FUFU
(POUNDED YAM)

Remember that song that says, "Chicken noodle soup with a soda on the side?" Growing up, my sisters and I remixed it to "fufu and soup with a Fanta on the side." Fufu, which is just yam that has been pounded into a powder, is a staple in African cuisine. Fufu is the most common swallow to accompany a soup dish. It's a heavy starch and can be very filling.

One of my favorite memories of my dad is watching him make fufu. He always used so much power and energy—I'd hear the pot banging on the stove over and over again. His fufu was always the fluffiest. A bowl of fufu, Egusi Soup (page 18) and an orange soda like Fanta is exactly how this meal should be enjoyed.

MAKES 2 TO 4 SERVINGS

2 cups (480 ml) water
2 cups (250 g) yam powder

Bring the water to a boil in a medium pot over high heat.

Once the water is boiling, add the yam powder and combine using a wooden spoon or fufu stick. Continue to mix the yam powder as it thickens. It's ready when the mixture is smooth and thickens to a "dough," 5 to 7 minutes. It should form a ball.

Serve with your soup of choice—fufu goes especially well with Egusi Soup (page 18) and Buchi's Okra Soup (page 34).

BANKU
(WHITE CORNMEAL SWALLOW)

While I love Fufu (page 49), the older I get the more I'm into exploring what other type of starches (or "swallows"; [page 166]) I can eat my soups with. One of my best friends is Ghanaian, and she loves banku. After hearing her talk so much about it, I grew curious and decided to make it on my own. It's quickly pushed Fufu out of the way for me, and I love enjoying it with a bowl of Buchi's Okra Soup (page 34).

MAKES 6 SERVINGS

6 cups (1 kg) white corn flour or white cornmeal

1 cup (240 ml) water, plus more as needed

In a large bowl, combine the corn flour with just enough warm water to dampen it, and mix together. Cover the bowl with a clean tea towel and set it in a warm place (e.g., near the oven, by the fireplace, on top of the refrigerator) for 2 to 3 days. This process allows the flour to ferment, and it should have a slightly sour aroma (like rising bread dough).

Transfer the fermented dough to a clean work surface. Knead the dough until it is mixed thoroughly and stiff, about 5 minutes.

Bring 1 cup (240 ml) of the water to a boil in a large pot over medium heat. Slowly begin adding the fermented dough gradually. Stir vigorously while continuing to add all of the dough. Cook for 20 minutes, stirring occasionally. It should become stiff. Form it into small balls about the size of a tennis ball.

Serve banku with your choice of soup.

CHIN CHIN

(FRIED DOUGH SNACKS)

If there is one snack I'm addicted to, chin chin is definitely the one. Whenever my grandparents would visit from Nigeria, they would always bring at least two suitcases filled with food for my mom and her brothers: sugarcane, Nigerian yams, spices and seasonings! Rest assured that in those suitcases were always bags of chin chin—sweet, crispy and crunchy dough seasoned with sugar and African nutmeg. Of course, we could make this snack at home, but there's just something about chin chin made in Nigeria that makes it taste even better. The perfect chin chin should be sweet but not cloying. This is my version.

MAKES 8 TO 10 SERVINGS

3 cups (375 g) all-purpose flour

1 tsp baking powder

½ tsp African nutmeg (ehuru)

¾ cup (144 g) sugar

½ cup (115 g) margarine, cut into pieces

⅓ cup (80 ml) milk

Vegetable oil, as needed

In a large bowl, combine the flour, baking powder, African nutmeg and sugar. Add the margarine a few pieces at a time and begin to combine until the mixture is crumbly.

Slowly add the milk until the dough becomes stretchy. Note that the dough should not be sticky, so take care to not add too much liquid.

Transfer the dough to a floured work surface. Roll the dough out to ¼ inch (6 mm) thick, then knead it into a ball. Divide the ball in half and roll out each half to ⅛ inch (3 mm) thick. Slice the dough into long strips that are ¼ inch (6 mm) wide. Cut the strips into small squares.

Heat the oil in a large pot to 375°F (191°F). Add the chin chin to the oil and fry for 3 minutes, turning about 1 to 2 minutes in, until they are golden brown and crisp.

Remove the chin chin from the oil with a slotted spoon and transfer them to a large baking sheet lined with paper towels.

Store chin chin in an airtight container for up to 1 month.

ERAN PAII
(NIGERIAN MEAT PIE)

Nigerian Meat Pie is moist and has a minced meat, potato and carrot filling. The seasoning of the filling is what gives it that unique taste, and if you're throwing a party, you better be sure to have a tray of these pies front and center. I love to watch my mum make the dough for these pies. I've taken her method and used it over and over again. It's foolproof.

MAKES 6 SERVINGS

FILLING

2 tbsp (30 ml) vegetable oil

1 medium onion, diced

1 lb (450 g) ground beef

2 beef bouillon cubes

1 tsp dried thyme

1⅓ cups (320 ml) water, divided

2 medium russet potatoes, chopped into bite-size pieces

2 medium carrots, chopped into bite-size pieces

2 tbsp (16 g) all-purpose flour

Salt, as needed

DOUGH

8 cups (1 kg) all-purpose flour

2 tsp (8 g) baking powder

Pinch of salt

1 lb (450 g) cold margarine, cut into tiny pieces

½ cup (120 ml) ice-cold water

1 large egg, beaten

Preheat the oven to 350°F (177°C). Spray a large baking sheet with oil.

To make the filling, heat the oil in a large skillet over medium-high heat. Add the onion and sauté until it is translucent, 2 to 3 minutes. Add the ground beef to the skillet, breaking it into pieces with a wooden spoon. As the meat begins to brown, add the bouillon cubes, thyme and 1 cup (240 ml) of the water.

Cover the skillet and bring the mixture to a boil. Once the meat is boiling, add the potatoes and carrots and cook until they are softened and most of the liquid has evaporated, about 10 minutes.

Dissolve the flour in the remaining ⅓ cup (80 ml) of water to make a slurry. Add this to the filling. Season the filling with salt and set it aside.

To make the dough, place the flour in a large bowl. Add the baking powder and salt. Mix the dry ingredients together, until well combined.

Add the margarine 1 tablespoon (14 g) at a time. Using your fingers, work the margarine into the flour until the mixture is quite crumbly. Add the ice cold water and combine.

Transfer the dough to a floured work surface. Knead the dough until you are able to form a ball, about 5 to 7 minutes. Roll the dough out until it is ¼ inch (6 mm) thick. Use a cookie cutter or a jar lid to cut out round pieces of dough. Set any excess dough aside.

Place 1 tablespoon (14 g) of the filling in the center of a dough circle. Rub the perimeter of the dough circle with the beaten egg. Fold one edge of the dough circle to the other edge and press the edges together to seal. Use a fork to crimp the edges together and brush the outside with the beaten egg. Repeat this process with the rest of the filling and dough circles.

Place the pies on the prepared baking sheet. Bake the pies for 30 to 40 minutes, until the dough has turned golden brown and is cooked all the way through. Allow the pies to rest for 5 minutes before serving.

SCOTCH EGG, NIGERIAN-STYLE

A lot of West African countries were influenced by England's colonialism, especially Nigeria. Nigeria didn't gain its independence from England until 1960, and you can still see English influences in the culture today. My grandad once told me the story of how he was forced to give all of his children English Christian names, an occurence that really impacted my mum when she gave birth to her own children. She made it a point to not give us any English names. While Scotch eggs aren't traditionally Nigerian, it definitely made a lasting impression on the country because it's quite common for breakfast. In Europe and America, the egg will often have a soft or runny yolk. In Nigeria, we boil the egg until it is hard, giving the inside a nice creamy texture while the outside is crisp and salty.

MAKES 4 SERVINGS

1 lb (450 g) ground pork sausage

½ tsp dried thyme

½ tsp dried rosemary

½ tsp cayenne pepper

½ tsp black pepper

½ tsp salt

1 beef bouillon cube

⅓ cup (42 g) all-purpose flour

½ cup (60 g) panko breadcrumbs

2 large eggs, beaten

8 medium hard-boiled eggs, peeled

Vegetable oil, as needed

In a medium bowl, combine the sausage, thyme, rosemary, cayenne, black pepper, salt and bouillon cube.

Set up a breading station by putting the flour, breadcrumbs and beaten eggs into three separate bowls.

Coat a boiled egg in flour, then take some sausage and wrap the egg in it completely.

Dip the sausage-wrapped egg into the flour, then the beaten eggs, then the breadcrumbs. Ensure that it is coated well with the breadcrumbs.

Repeat this process with the remaining eggs and set them aside.

Heat the oil in a large pot until it reaches 350°F (177°C). Fry the Scotch eggs until they turn golden brown, 5 to 7 minutes.

Remove the eggs from the oil and serve immediately.

NIGERIAN SALAD

This is no ordinary salad. When I think of Nigerian Salad, I instantly think of a full-course meal. That's because this salad is *packed* with filling ingredients. From baked beans to boiled eggs to an array of vegetables, this isn't the type of salad you eat if you're watching your diet. There's a secret (well, not-so-secret) ingredient that goes into this salad, Heinz Salad Cream, and if it's missing . . . well, then, you end up with just a regular salad. Heinz Salad Cream is a must for Nigerian Salad. It gives the salad that creamy, tangy taste and it is wildly addicting.

MAKES 4 TO 6 SERVINGS

2 large carrots, peeled and shredded

½ large head lettuce, shredded or finely chopped

½ large head green cabbage, shredded or finely chopped

1 large tomato, roughly chopped

1 medium cucumber, roughly chopped

1 large red onion, thinly sliced

½ (14-oz [392-g]) can Heinz brand baked beans

½ (15-oz [420-g]) can sweet corn, drained

2 large hard-boiled eggs, peeled and sliced

Heinz Salad Cream, for serving

In a large bowl, combine the carrots, lettuce, cabbage, tomato, cucumber, onion, baked beans and sweet corn. Mix the salad together until it's well combined, cover the bowl with plastic wrap and place it in the fridge to chill for 1 hour.

When you are ready to serve the salad, remove it from the fridge and toss it again.

Place the eggs on top and serve with the Heinz Salad Cream.

AKARA
(LABOR-OF-LOVE BLACK-EYED PEA FRITTERS)

One of my dad's favorite breakfasts that my mum would make for him is akara and bread. Making these fritters is a true testament of love, because the process is truly laborious. It starts by soaking the black-eyed peas in water overnight to loosen the peels. Then comes the task of peeling the peas so that the black "eye" is removed. I never understood why Mum couldn't just blend it all together, but she always reminded us that there are no shortcuts in the kitchen: having the black specks in these fritters is unattractive and does alter the taste a little. Watching my mum work so hard to prepare these for us always made them taste better. Love is one of the best ingredients you can put into a meal. These may be labor intensive, but are worth the effort every time. The outside is crispy and inside is a soft, fluffy texture full of flavor.

MAKES 4 TO 6 SERVINGS

1 cup (151 g) dried black-eyed peas

¼ cup (60 ml) water

1 medium red bell pepper, roughly chopped

1 small habanero chile, stem removed

1 small onion, roughly chopped

Salt, to taste

Vegetable oil, for frying

Bread, for serving

Soak the black-eyed peas overnight in water. The next day, peel the beans so that the black "eye" is removed.

In a blender, combine the peeled beans, water, bell pepper, habanero and onion. Blend until the mixture is smooth.

Pour the batter into a medium bowl and season the batter with salt. Stir to combine.

Heat 3 to 4 cups (720 to 960 ml) of the oil in large pot until it reaches 350°F (177°C).

Once the oil is hot, use a spoon to scoop and carefully drop the batter into the oil. Fry the fritters on each side until they are golden brown, about 5 minutes total.

Remove the fritters from the oil with a slotted spoon and transfer them to a plate lined with paper towels.

Serve with your choice of bread.

NOTE: My mum made a large batch of these once for my childhood best friend and her family. My friend came back to me and let me know how much she loved them and that she enjoyed dipping them in mustard. Naturally, we thought the combination very strange, but once I tried it, I discovered that I loved it. Try it if you dare!

MUM'S MOIN MOIN
(SPICY BEAN CAKES)

Moin moin is like a savory steamed bean cake, slightly spicy from the pepper and nutty from the palm oil. My mum's moin moin is a family favorite. From my dad to her brothers to family friends, if they know she is throwing a get-together, her moin moin is always requested by everyone. I feel closest to my mum when I'm in the kitchen with her. We aren't too much alike. We both love to cook, obviously, and I definitely learned how to work hard from her, but that's about it. We don't get to cook together often since I live in LA now—it's something I miss a lot. Making her moin moin makes me feel accomplished, like I am a strong, independent, loving and nurturing African woman.

MAKES 4 TO 6 SERVINGS

1 cup (151 g) dried black-eyed peas

½ cup (76 g) roughly chopped onion

½ large red bell pepper

1 small habanero chile, stem removed

1 chicken bouillon cube

2 tsp (10 g) salt

2 tbsp (30 ml) palm oil

¼ cup (60 ml) vegetable oil

1 tsp cayenne pepper

2 tbsp (12 g) ground crayfish

3 large hard-boiled eggs, peeled and halved

1 cup (230 g) canned corned beef

Soak the black-eyed peas overnight in water. Once the beans have soaked, remove the skins of the beans. Reserve the soaking water.

In a food processor, combine the beans, onion, bell pepper, habanero and 1 cup (240 ml) of the soaking water. Process until the ingredients are completely smooth.

Pour the mixture into a large bowl and add the bouillon cube, salt, palm oil, vegetable oil, cayenne and ground crayfish. Mix until combined.

Pour the mixture into heatproof ramekins, filling ¾ way. Leave about ¼ space since more goes on top. Traditionally, moin moin is wrapped in banana leaves. If you can't get your hands on banana leaves, you can make aluminum foil packets by cutting a square of foil, folding it in half and sealing the bottom and sides by folding them over 1 inch (3 cm). Using ramekins is the easiest way, however.

To each ramekin, add half of an egg and a spoonful of corned beef before pouring a little more of the blended mixture on top.

Pour about ½ inch (13 mm) of water into the bottom of a large pot over medium-low heat. Place a steamer rack in the bottom of the pot so the ramekins are not sitting directly in the water. Gently place the ramekins on top of the steamer rack and cover the pot with a lid.

Steam for 45 to 60 minutes.

Serve immediately.

KOKI
(AFRICAN CORN TAMALES)

My discovery of this dish comes from my love of corn. One of my Cameroonian friends made koki for me once, and my taste buds were blown away. Who knew Africans had their own version of corn tamales? This is her recipe; though, over the years I've adapted it as my own by the amount of spinach I've added in. Her recipe calls for 1 cup (30 g), while mine has 4 cups (120 g). I love the texture the additional spinach adds, and any excuse to add some extra greens is always good with me!

MAKES 4 TO 6 SERVINGS

¾ cup (180 ml) palm oil

4 cups (577 g) fresh corn kernels

½ large onion, finely chopped

1 small habanero chile, stem removed

¾ cup (180 ml) water, divided

1 cup (170 g) yellow cornmeal

2 tsp (10 g) salt

1 chicken or vegetable bouillon cube

4 cups (120 g) loosely packed spinach, roughly chopped

6 large banana leaves, soaked in hot water to soften and rinsed thoroughly (see note)

Heat the oil in a large skillet over medium heat for 2 minutes. You just want to heat up the oil—take care not to bleach the oil. Set the skillet aside.

In a blender, combine the corn, onion, habanero and ¼ cup (60 ml) of the water and blend the ingredients to a coarsely ground paste. Pour the mixture into a large bowl and add the cornmeal, heated oil, salt and bouillon cube. Mix well, then add the spinach and mix again until the ingredients are well incorporated.

Pour the remaining ½ cup (120 ml) of water into the bottom of a large pot. Place a steamer rack in the bottom of the pot. Bring the water to a gentle boil over medium-high heat.

Take 2 spoonfuls of the corn mixture and place them in a banana leaf. Wrap the leaf over the mixture. Once it is wrapped, fold both ends inward and place the tamale directly on top of the steamer rack seam-side down. Do this with the remaining mixture and banana leaves.

Once all the tamales are in the pot, cover the pot and steam the tamales for 30 minutes. Check the pot periodically. If all the water dries up before the 30 minutes is up, add more. Take care that you are not pouring the water directly on top of the leaves.

Let the tamales rest 10 minutes before serving.

NOTE: If you cannot find banana leaves, feel free to substitute them with aluminum foil.

AFRICAN YAM FRIES

What's an African French fry? Instead of fries made with potatoes, try them made with yam. My mum used to make these all the time, and instead of enjoying them with ketchup, we dipped them into Nigerian Red Stew (page 14).

MAKES 4 SERVINGS

½ a medium yam

2 tbsp (16 g) all-purpose flour

2 tbsp (30 ml) water

1 large egg

Salt, as needed

Vegetable oil, as needed

Pili Pili (page 41), for serving

Peel the yam, removing the rough outer skin. Cut the yam into round pieces and wash them thoroughly. Add the yam to a large pot filled with water. Cover the pot and boil the yam over high heat for 10 minutes, or just until the yam begins to soften. Drain the yam and allow it to cool before cutting it into French fries.

In a large bowl, mix together the flour, water and egg. Add some salt for seasoning.

Gently add the yam fries to the batter and coat them evenly with it.

Heat some oil to 375°F (191°C) in a large pot. Once the oil has heated, carefully drop in the fries. You may have to do this in batches to avoid crowding the pot and bringing down the temperature of the oil. Fry the yam fries until they are golden brown, 5 to 7 minutes.

Remove the fries from the oil and season them with more salt.

Serve with Pili Pili, ketchup or the condiment of your choice.

PUFF PUFF
(NIGERIAN DOUGHNUTS)

These puff puff are a very popular street-food snack in Nigeria. I have so many good memories of snacking on these soft, chewy and sweet delicious balls of deep-fried dough. Because they were such a treat, I usually had to wait until a party before I could have one; so as soon as I got old enough, I bugged my mom for the recipe and started making them on my own.

Traditionally, these teeter between sweet and savory (leaning more toward the sweet side). In my family, we like to make them extra sweet, so vanilla extract goes into the batter and as soon as they come out of the hot oil, I like to sprinkle powdered sugar over them for that next level of sweetness. These little treats are perfect for any time of the day. We have them in the morning or afternoon with a hot cup of tea, and of course these make their way onto the table at any party or function.

MAKES 4 TO 6 SERVINGS

1 (¼-oz [7-g]) packet active dry yeast

1 cup (192 g) granulated sugar

1 tsp vanilla extract

¼ tsp ground nutmeg

1 tsp salt

2 cups (480 ml) warm water

3½ cups (438 g) all-purpose flour

Vegetable oil, as needed

Powdered sugar, optional

In a small bowl, mix together the yeast, granulated sugar, vanilla, nutmeg, salt and water. Set aside for 5 minutes. Place the flour in a large bowl.

Gradually begin adding the water mixture to the flour and mix together by hand. The consistency of the mixture should resemble a thick pancake batter. If you find the batter is too thick, you can adjust the amount of water as necessary.

Cover the bowl with a tea towel and set it aside for 1 to 2 hours in a cool, dark, dry area while the batter begins to rise.

After the mixture has risen considerably, fill a large pot with the oil to a depth of 3 inches (8 cm). (Too little oil will result in flat doughnuts.) Heat the oil to 350°F (177°C) over medium heat.

Once the oil is hot, carefully drop the batter into the oil with an ice cream scoop. Alternatively, place the batter into a piping bag, and as you begin to squeeze some of the batter out, snip it off with a pair of kitchen scissors into the oil. This is the easiest way to get the classic round shape if you are not able to do so by hand.

Fry the doughnuts for 3 to 5 minutes, until the dough is a golden-brown color. The doughnuts should rise to the top. You may need to flip them so the other side can cook.

Remove the puff puff with tongs or a slotted spoon and place them on paper towels to absorb the oil. Sprinkle them with powdered sugar (if using). Serve immediately.

KUNNU AYA
(TIGERNUT MILK)

There's something so satisfying about making your own milk: the process of soaking the nuts, then pressing the mixture through the nut-milk bag for a sweet and delicious milk. I make this whenever I crave simplicity and comfort.

MAKES 4 CUPS (960 ML)

8 oz (224 g) raw organic tigernuts

1 (2- to 4-inch [6- to 10-cm]) cinnamon stick

4 cups (960 ml) warm water

3 cardamom pods

½ cup (110 g) organic jaggery

Place the tigernuts and cinnamon stick in a large mixing bowl and cover them with the water. Soak the nuts anywhere from 12 to 24 hours, until they are soft.

Pour the entire contents of the bowl into a blender, along with the cardamom pods and jaggery. Blend until the milk is smooth. You may need to add more water if you find the mixture to be too thick.

Transfer the milk to the fridge and allow it to rest for 1 hour.

Spoon the milk into a nut-milk bag, and press the milk through the bag into glasses filled with ice.

UNIVERSITY CHAPMAN

This is a party in your mouth! The first time I had Chapman was at an African restaurant my freshman year in university. It was my first taste of freedom, partying with other Africans my age without the watchful eyes of my parents, uncles and aunties. I'd always seen adults ordering Chapman, but had never had it myself. I instantly fell in love with the bright, sweet and fruity taste of Chapman and to my surprise there was no alcohol, making it the perfect mocktail!

MAKES 4 SERVINGS

2 cups (480 ml) orange soda (I recommend Fanta)

2 cups (480 ml) lemon lime soda (I recommend Sprite)

⅓ cup (80 ml) concentrated black currant juice (I recommend Ribena)

¼ cup (60 ml) grenadine syrup

1 tsp angostura bitters

1 large orange, sliced

Juice of 1 lime

1 large lime, sliced

8 to 10 ice cubes

In a large punch bowl, combine the orange soda, lemon lime soda, concentrated black currant juice, grenadine syrup, angostura bitters, orange slices, lime juice, lime slices and ice cubes. Stir the ingredients together and pour into glasses filled with ice.

EASTERN AFRICA

Eastern Africa is unique because it's a large, diverse region where indigenous ingredients and recipes are the most popular. A lot of recipes come from the Maasai, who are known for eating cow's milk and corn, while other influences are from India and Arab countries. With so many diverse influences, Eastern Africa gives us a wide range of flavors. My favorite parts of East African cuisines are the spices and homemade bread recipes like Chapati (page 96) and Injera (page 99) made to eat with stews like Doro Wot (page 77). Mostly farm-rich cuisine, a lot of East African recipes will include beef and vegetables.

DORO WOT

(ETHIOPIAN CHICKEN STEW)

Stews that take a really long time to cook—I'm talking low-and-slow—are my favorites. This style of cooking allows all of the ingredients to hang out in one pot and cook together, maximizing the flavors. This Doro Wot is just that: chicken simmered in berbere spices and a flavorful broth just begging to be wrapped up in Injera (page 99). This is the dish I always order at Ethiopian restaurants, and since I learned to make it at home, it's a regular dish in my dinner rotation.

MAKES 4 TO 6 SERVINGS

2½ lb (1.1 kg) chicken thighs

Salt and black pepper, as needed

3 tbsp (42 g) butter

2 medium onions, thinly sliced

¼ cup (60 ml) canola oil

1 tbsp (9 g) roughly chopped garlic

1 tsp minced fresh ginger

½ tbsp (4 g) paprika

2 tbsp (16 g) Berbere Spice Mix (page 78)

3 cups (720 g) water

1 tbsp (10 g) tomato paste

6 large soft-boiled eggs, peeled

Rice or Injera (page 99), for serving

Season the chicken thighs with salt and black pepper.

Heat a large pot over medium-high heat. Add the butter and allow it to melt. Add the onions and sauté just until they are caramelized, about 10 minutes.

Add the oil to the pot, followed by the garlic, ginger, paprika and Berbere Spice Mix. Stir to combine and cook for 2 to 3 minutes.

Add the water to the pot, followed by the chicken thighs and tomato paste. Bring the mixture to a boil.

Cover the pot, reduce the heat to medium-low and cook for 30 minutes, stirring occasionally.

Carefully add the eggs to the stew and cook for 10 more minutes.

Serve immediately with rice or Injera.

TSEBHI BIRSEN

(ERITREAN RED LENTILS WITH BERBERE SPICE MIX)

Berbere is the spice of East Africa! The first time I had Ethiopian food, I was blown away—there were so many side dishes filled with colorful vegetables and meats that I was in awe. I knew I wanted to dive deeper into the culture, so my first lesson was how to make this Berbere Spice Mix. It's used to season a large array of Ethiopian and Eritrean dishes, from chicken to beef to stews to vegetables.

I always keep a jar of this spice mix in my spice cabinet, especially for when I prepare Eritrean red lentils. The spices give the lentils heat and so much flavor. Adding coconut milk and cinnamon brings in a little sweetness for a perfect marriage of heat and sweet. A bowl of these lentils is like a bowl of comfort, and they will stick to your ribs in a good way.

MAKES 4 TO 6 SERVINGS

BERBERE SPICE MIX

1 tsp coriander seeds

1 tsp cardamom seeds

1 tsp fenugreek seeds

3 tbsp (24 g) smoked paprika

1 tbsp (8 g) cayenne pepper

2 tsp (6 g) ground cumin

1 tsp ground turmeric

1 tsp freshly ground black peppercorns

½ tsp ground cloves

½ tsp ground allspice

½ tsp ground ginger

½ tsp ground cinnamon

1 tsp salt

LENTILS

2 tbsp (30 ml) olive oil

1 large onion, diced

3 tbsp (24 g) Berbere Spice Mix

4 large tomatoes, diced

1 tbsp (10 g) tomato paste

½ tsp minced fresh ginger

1 tsp curry powder

½ tsp ground cinnamon

1½ cups (302 g) red lentils, washed and drained

2 cups (480 ml) coconut milk

Salt and black pepper, to taste

Aunty Bernie's Chapati (page 96) or rice, for serving

(continued)

TSEBHI BIRSEN (CONT.)

To make the Berbere Spice Mix, lightly toast the coriander seeds, cardamom seeds and fenugreek seeds in a skillet over medium-high heat for 2 to 3 minutes.

Grind all of the berbere spices together in a mortar and pestle or spice grinder. Transfer the spice mix to an airtight container and use as needed.

To make the lentils, heat the oil in a large pot over medium-high heat. Add the onion and sauté for 2 to 3 minutes, until it becomes translucent.

Add the Berbere Spice Mix to the onion, stirring constantly. Cook for 5 minutes and then add the tomatoes and tomato paste. Cook for 4 to 5 minutes.

Add the ginger, curry powder and cinnamon and stir to combine.

Add the lentils, stirring constantly. Let the lentils toast for about 1 minute.

Add the coconut milk. (You may need to add some water so that the lentils are completely submerged in liquid.)

Bring the mixture to a boil, reduce the heat to medium-low and cover the pot.

Simmer the lentils for 45 minutes, until they are soft and most of the liquid has evaporated. Season with salt and black pepper. Serve with Aunty Bernie's Chapati or rice.

BEEF SAMOSAS

Eastern Africa has a lot of Indian influences. From curries to roti to spiced chai, you'll see similarities in a lot of the recipes. I believe samosas were introduced to East Africa by way of India; but like in most cultures, no two recipes are ever exactly the same. These pockets of dough are filled with a spiced beef filling and peas. You won't be able to eat just one.

MAKES 4 TO 6 SERVINGS

DOUGH

4 cups (500 g) all-purpose flour, plus more as needed

1 tsp salt

4 tbsp (60 ml) vegetable oil, plus more as needed

1½ cups (360 ml) warm water

FILLING

1 lb (450 g) ground beef

1 cup (150 g) frozen peas, thawed

1 small white onion, finely chopped

5 cloves garlic, minced

2 tsp (6 g) grated fresh ginger

1 medium jalapeño chile, minced

1 tsp ground turmeric

1 tsp ground cumin

1 tsp ground coriander

½ tsp ground cardamom

½ tsp ground cinnamon

Salt and black pepper, as needed

Vegetable oil, as needed

To make the dough, mix together the flour, salt and oil in a large bowl until the mixture is crumbly.

Gradually add the water while mixing it with the flour. Knead the dough for 20 minutes by hand until you get a soft and smooth dough. The dough should not be sticky.

Put the dough in a greased container and allow it to rest for 1 hour at room temperature.

Divide the dough into 4 equal balls. On a floured work surface, roll out each ball of dough into a circle 10 to 12 inches (25 to 30 cm) in diameter. Brush some oil on the dough's surface and lightly sprinkle it with flour. Repeat this process with the remaining balls of dough.

Heat a large skillet over medium heat and place a dough circle in the skillet. Cook for 1 to 2 minutes per side (just until the dough starts to bubble up). You are not going to cook the dough all the way.

Transfer the partially cooked dough to a cutting board and cut it into 4 equal parts to form semi-triangular pieces. Separate the triangles and cover them with a clean tea towel until you are ready to fill them. Repeat this process with the remaining dough circles.

To make the filling, heat a large skillet over medium-high heat. Add the ground beef, breaking it up with a wooden spoon. Add the peas, onion, garlic, ginger, jalapeño, turmeric, cumin, coriander, cardamom, cinnamon and salt and black pepper to the beef.

(continued)

BEEF SAMOSAS (CONT.)

Cook the meat until it is completely brown and all of the pink is gone, 10 to 15 minutes. Remove the skillet from the heat, set it aside and allow the filling to cool completely.

To assemble the samosas, fold the dough triangles into a cone shape. Fill each cone with 1 tablespoon (14 g) of the beef filling. Take care to not overfill the cones. Seal the cones by pressing the ends together.

Heat some oil in large pot until it reaches 350°F (177°C). Fry the samosas in batches until they are a deep golden-brown color, 5 to 7 minutes.

Serve with the chutney (page 164) of your choice.

MUAMBA DE GALINHA

(MUAMBA CHICKEN)

I was pleasantly surprised to find out that other regions in Africa love to use palm oil almost as much as West Africans. This chicken stew hails from Angola, and the palm oil is the true star of this dish. It's what gives it that red color. Growing up, we always ate palm oil sparingly as it can cause health issues if eaten in excess. Whenever I yearn for the taste of palm oil, I always make this stew.

MAKES 4 TO 6 SERVINGS

2 lb (900 g) chicken (any cut), cut into bite-size pieces

Juice of ½ lemon

1 tsp minced garlic

1 tsp dried thyme

1 tsp black pepper

2 tsp (4 g) smoked paprika, divided

2 tsp (10 g) salt, plus more as needed

1 chicken bouillon cube

¼ cup (60 ml) canola oil

¼ cup (60 ml) palm oil

4 cloves garlic, minced

2 medium onions, sliced

1 small habanero chile, stem removed

2 large tomatoes, diced

2 cups (480 ml) chicken stock

1 tsp white pepper

¾ lb (338 g) cubed butternut squash

½ cup (120 ml) water

20 pieces okra, sliced in half

Rice, for serving

To make the chicken, place the chicken pieces in a large bowl. Add the lemon juice and toss the pieces to coat. Season the chicken with the garlic, thyme, black pepper, 1 teaspoon of smoked paprika, salt and bouillon cube. Mix the ingredients together well, ensuring that the chicken is completely coated with all of the seasonings.

Heat the canola oil and palm oil in a large saucepan over medium-high heat. Add the chicken and brown it on all sides, about 1 to 2 minutes per side.

To make the stew, add the garlic, onions, habanero and tomatoes to the saucepan and sauté for 3 to 5 minutes.

Next, add the chicken stock, remaining smoked paprika and white pepper. Stir to combine and bring the mixture to a boil. Once the stew is boiling, add the butternut squash, water and more salt. Reduce the heat to medium-low and simmer for 20 minutes, allowing the stew to thicken.

Add the okra and cook for an additional 5 minutes.

Serve the stew with rice.

PILAU
(KENYAN SPICED RICE)

If I had to choose my last meal on Earth, it would definitely be a rice dish. This pilau is one of my best rice recipes! I tried to capture the essence of East African flavors by including cumin, cardamom, curry powder and star anise. This recipe is aromatic and packed with flavor.

MAKES 4 TO 6 SERVINGS

1 cup (240 ml) vegetable oil

1 large onion, diced

4 cloves garlic, minced

2 tsp (6 g) minced fresh ginger

½ tsp smoked paprika

1 tsp ground cumin

½ tsp ground cardamom

½ tsp curry powder

2 medium tomatoes, roughly chopped

4 medium Yukon gold potatoes, peeled and diced

2 cups (422 g) basmati rice

4 cups (960 ml) chicken stock

1 (2- to 4-inch [6- to 10-cm]) cinnamon stick

½ tsp ground star anise

1 bay leaf

Salt and black pepper, to taste

Kachumbari (page 92), for serving

Heat the oil in a large pot over medium-high heat. Add the onion and fry just until it starts to turn golden brown, about 5 minutes. Add the garlic, ginger, smoked paprika, cumin, cardamom and curry powder and sauté for 10 minutes.

Add the tomatoes, potatoes and rice to the pot. Stir together and cook for 5 minutes.

Add the chicken stock to the pot, along with the cinnamon stick, star anise and bay leaf. Season with the salt and black pepper, cover the pot and simmer for 30 minutes, until all the liquid has evaporated.

Fluff the rice with a fork and serve alongside Kachumbari.

MTUZI WA SAMAKI
(FISH IN COCONUT CURRY)

There's something really special about the combination of coconut and curry. It's so hearty, comforting and delicious. There's a hint of heat and spice from the curry, accompanied by coconut milk, which brings a nice balance of sweetness and creaminess. Whenever I'm having a bad day, all I need to do is make some of this coconut curry and a smile instantly hits my face. Make this coconut curry whenever you feel like you need some comfort. I call it a hug from a bowl.

MAKES 4 TO 6 SERVINGS

1 (1-lb [450-g]) halibut fillet, skin removed

1 tbsp (8 g) plus ¾ tsp curry powder, divided

1 tsp salt, plus more as needed

1 tsp black pepper, plus more as needed

1 tbsp (15 ml) canola oil, plus more as needed

1 medium onion, diced

2 medium bell peppers (any color), diced

2 tsp (6 g) minced fresh ginger

3 cloves garlic, minced

2 large tomatoes, roughly chopped

2 tbsp (30 ml) fresh lemon juice

1 cup (240 ml) coconut milk

1 small bunch fresh cilantro, roughly chopped, for garnish

4 lemon wedges, for garnish

Season both sides of the halibut with ¾ teaspoon of the curry powder, the 1 teaspoon of salt and the 1 teaspoon of black pepper.

Heat the oil in a large saucepan over medium-high heat. Add the halibut to the saucepan and sear both sides for 2 minutes each. Remove the fish from the saucepan and set it aside.

Add some more oil to the saucepan. Add the onion and bell peppers and sauté until the onion is translucent, 2 to 3 minutes. Add the ginger and garlic and sauté until they are fragrant, about 30 seconds. Add the remaining 1 tablespoon (8 g) of curry powder, salt, black pepper, tomatoes and lemon juice. Reduce the heat to medium-low and cook until the tomatoes break down, 5 to 7 minutes. You can use a wooden spoon to speed up this process. Next, add the coconut milk and stir the ingredients together.

Add the fish, along with its juices, back to the saucepan. Reduce the heat to low, cover the saucepan and simmer for 10 minutes.

Garnish the dish with the cilantro and serve with the lemon wedges.

SUPU VIAZI
(TANZANIA'S COCONUT POTATO SOUP)

This coconut potato soup is rich and creamy. It has an underlying taste of coconut that doesn't leave the soup tasting sweet, just deliciously velvety. The potatoes and green banana add some starch and are quite filling since this soup lacks any meat. It's even better when you add sliced avocados on top! You can serve this as a meal on its own or as a starter before any other meal.

MAKES 4 TO 6 SERVINGS

2 tbsp (30 ml) vegetable oil

1 large onion, diced

4 cloves garlic, minced

1 large green bell pepper, diced

2 large carrots, diced

2 large tomatoes, diced

6 medium Yukon gold potatoes, cubed

1 large green banana, cubed

1 (14-oz [420-ml]) can coconut milk

4 cups (960 ml) water

Salt and black pepper, to taste

1 large avocado, pitted, peeled and sliced, for serving

Heat the oil in a large pot over medium-high heat. Add the onion and garlic and cook until the onion is translucent, 2 to 3 minutes. Add the bell pepper and carrots and sauté for 5 to 10 minutes.

Add the tomatoes and cook for 10 to 15 minutes. Most of the liquid should evaporate.

Add the potatoes, banana, coconut milk and water. Stir the ingredients together and season with the salt and black pepper.

Reduce the heat to medium-low, cover the pot and simmer for 30 minutes.

Serve the soup with the slices of avocado on top.

KACHUMBARI
(EAST AFRICAN SALSA)

This is the one condiment I have with almost all of my meals. It resembles pico de gallo and is perfect for some acidity, crunch and heat to go along with rice and stews. Most Kenyan and Tanzanian meals will include this salsa (or salad, as some refer to it) on the side. Its colors are so vibrant, and it really brings a burst of flavor to your mouth. Serve this alongside Pilau (page 87), roasted meats or Bhajias (page 95).

**MAKES 4 TO
6 SERVINGS**

2 large tomatoes, diced

½ large red onion, diced

2 large jalapeño chiles, seeded and diced

1 medium cucumber, diced

2 cloves garlic, minced

Juice of 1 lime

½ cup (20 g) fresh cilantro, roughly chopped

Salt and black pepper, to taste

In a small bowl, combine the tomatoes, onion, jalapeños, cucumber, garlic, lime juice and cilantro. Season with the salt and black pepper.

Serve the salsa alongside the meal of your choice.

BHAJIAS
(FRIES)

Here's another "French fry" recipe—except this time, potatoes are used instead of yam. I love to season potatoes heavily because they absorb a lot of flavor. I first had bhajias at one of my favorite Ethiopian restaurants when I lived in Atlanta. I loved how heavily seasoned the potatoes were. This is a real flavor bomb!

MAKES 4 SERVINGS

½ cup (65 g) gram flour

1 tbsp (11 g) corn flour

1 tsp minced ginger

2 tsp (6 g) ground cumin

1 tsp Pili Pili (page 41) or store-bought hot sauce

Salt, to taste

½ cup (20 g) finely chopped fresh cilantro

⅓ cup (80 ml) water

2 large russet potatoes

Vegetable oil, as needed

Kachumbari (page 92), for serving

In a large bowl, combine the gram flour, corn flour, ginger, cumin, Pili Pili, salt and cilantro.

Add the water to the flour mixture gradually. A thick paste should form and should coat the back of a spoon.

Using a sharp knife or mandoline, slice the potatoes very thin.

Add the potatoes to the flour mixture, making sure each slice is coated evenly.

Heat some oil in a large skillet over high heat. Fry the bhajias in the oil until they turn golden brown, 3 to 4 minutes.

Remove the bhajias from the oil with a slotted spoon and transfer them to a large baking sheet lined with paper towels.

Serve the bhajias with Kachumbari.

AUNTY BERNIE'S CHAPATI
(FLATBREAD)

My aunt, my mum's sister-in-law, is from Kenya. The first time Kenyan food was introduced to me was through her. She made this chapati bread to go along with a mung bean stew, and it was one of the best things I had ever tasted. I've never forgotten that meal, and whenever I see her I always request it.

**MAKES 4 TO
6 SERVINGS**

1 tsp salt

1 tsp sugar

2 tbsp (30 ml) vegetable oil, plus more as needed

1½ cups (360 ml) warm water, plus more as needed

3 cups (375 g) all-purpose flour

In a medium bowl, mix together the salt, sugar, oil and water. Stir until the sugar dissolves.

Place the flour in a large bowl. Slowly begin adding the liquid mixture to the flour, mixing well. Keep adding the liquid mixture until the dough is soft. Knead the dough for 5 minutes, adding water if needed.

Transfer the dough to a floured work surface and knead for an additional 10 minutes. The dough should be slightly elastic.

Return the dough to the bowl, adding a little vegetable oil and kneading it together. Cover the dough with plastic wrap and allow it to rest for 40 to 60 minutes.

After the dough has rested, divide the dough into 12 equal balls.

Roll each ball into a flat circular shape. Brush it with a little oil, and roll the chapati away from you. Once it is about 8 to 10 inches (20 to 25 cm) in diameter, coil the dough, rolling it into a pinwheel and making a coiled ball. Press the dough flat. You will still see some of the rings in the dough. This is fine. Roll this out into a flat circular shape.

Heat some oil in a large skillet over medium-high heat. Add a chapati and fry each side of the chapati until it is golden brown, 5 to 7 minutes total.

Serve the chapati with the soup or stew of your choice.

INJERA
(SOURDOUGH CREPES)

If you've had Ethiopian food, then you know you can't enjoy it without injera. I've honestly never seen a piece of flatbread, crepe or pancake so big that could easily hold 6 to 8 different side dishes and stews. It's magical in a way. I've tried my hand at making injera at home the classic way and it is really difficult. Many failed and frustrated attempts have led me to this simpler, humbler version of injera. While it may not hold up as authentic in Ethiopia, I happen to think it does just the trick, and my Ethiopian friends have agreed with me.

MAKES 4 TO 6 SERVINGS

¼ cup (33 g) teff flour
¾ cup (94 g) all-purpose flour
1 cup (240 ml) water
½ tsp salt
Vegetable oil, as needed

Place the teff flour in a medium bowl. Sift in the all-purpose flour.

Gradually begin adding the water to the flour mixture, stirring to avoid lumps.

Cover the bowl with a tea towel and set aside for 2 to 3 days. This allows the batter to ferment and develop that sour taste injera is known for.

After the batter has fermented, add the salt.

Heat a large nonstick skillet over medium-low heat. Brush the skillet with the oil.

Coat the skillet with a thin layer of the batter. You want it to be slightly thicker than a crepe but not as thick as a pancake.

Cook the injera until holes appear on the surface, 2 to 3 minutes. Once the surface is dry, remove the injera from the skillet. Repeat this process with the remaining batter.

Serve injera with any stew.

SUMMERTIME MANGO LEMONADE

Usually my grandparents would visit during summer, and I never wanted it to end. My sisters and I would often sit around the dining table as my dad would cut up mangoes for us to eat. I always had the hardest time peeling and cutting mangoes, and my sister Oreva would always try to keep the mango seeds. One time, I caught her trying to bury a mango seed in the Georgia red clay, hoping that a mango tree would sprout with juicy, fresh mangoes. Of course, that didn't happen, but we always had plenty of mangoes to make delicious mango lemonade.

MAKES 4 CUPS (960 ML)

2 cups (165 g) roughly chopped, extremely ripe mango

½ cup (120 ml) fresh lemon juice

2 tbsp (30 ml) fresh lime juice

¾ cup (180 ml) simple syrup

2 cups (480 ml) water, divided

½ cup (120 ml) moscato, optional

Fresh mint leaves, to taste

Ice cubes, as needed

Place the mango, lemon juice, lime juice, simple syrup and 1 cup (240 ml) of the water in a blender. Blend until smooth.

Pour the contents of the blender into a large pitcher. Add the remaining 1 cup (240 ml) of water, moscato (if using), mint leaves and ice. Stir to combine.

Pour the lemonade into glasses filled with ice cubes.

ST. JOHN THE BAPTIST PARISH LIBRARY
2920 NEW HIGHWAY 51
LAPLACE, LOUISIANA 70068

ST. JOHN THE BAPTIST PARISH LIBRARY
2920 NEW HIGHWAY 51
LAPLACE, LOUISIANA 70068

VITUMBUA
(COCONUT RICE PANCAKES)

I am not a huge sweets person, but for breakfast, I love to indulge. Ever since I was young I've loved all things coconut and caramel, and I would always top my pancakes or waffles with coconut flakes and caramel syrup. When I discovered vitumbua, it was like I died and went to heaven. Think of the fluffiest, sweetest pancakes on the inside with a crispy, caramelized exterior. These pancakes are truly special.

MAKES 4 TO 6 SERVINGS

COCONUT RICE PANCAKES

2 cups (422 g) jasmine rice

1 cup (240 ml) canned coconut milk

3 tbsp (14 g) raw unsweetened coconut flakes

1 tsp salt

1 cup (192 g) coconut sugar

1 tsp cardamom pods, crushed

1 tsp ground nutmeg

½ tsp almond extract

1 tsp active dry yeast

COCONUT SAUCE

1 (14-oz [420-ml]) can coconut milk

½ tsp vanilla extract

¾ cup (108 g) brown sugar

To make the coconut rice pancakes, soak the rice in large bowl of water overnight.

Drain the soaking water and add the rice to a blender with the coconut milk, coconut flakes, salt, coconut sugar, cardamom, nutmeg, almond extract and yeast. Blend the ingredients together until they are completely smooth.

Pour the batter into a large bowl and cover it with a tea towel. Allow the batter to rise for 2 hours. It's ready when you see bubbles forming.

Heat your appam pan (stuffed-pancake pan) over medium heat. Spray each cavity with cooking spray. When the pan is hot, fill each cavity about three-quarters full. Cook for 2 minutes, then flip and cook for 2 minutes on the other side.

Repeat this process until all the batter is gone.

To make the coconut sauce, bring the coconut milk, vanilla and brown sugar to a boil in a medium pot over medium heat. Reduce the heat to medium-low and cook the sauce, stirring constantly to avoid burning, for 20 minutes, until the sauce thickens and a caramel forms.

Serve the vitumbua with the coconut sauce.

MANDAZI
(KENYAN DOUGHNUTS)

Almost every culture has a doughnut recipe. Meet the Kenyan version. These remind me of beignets from New Orleans, especially because of the shape. What's different is the taste. These "doughnuts" are made with coconut milk and cardamom: a match made in heaven! Fry up a batch of these and serve them with chai tea.

MAKES 4 TO 6 SERVINGS

¼ cup (60 ml) warm water

½ cup (120 ml) canned coconut milk

¾ cup (144 g) sugar

2 tsp (6 g) active dry yeast

1 large egg

3 cups (375 g) all-purpose flour

1 tsp salt

1 tsp cardamom seeds, crushed

½ tsp ground nutmeg

½ tsp ground cinnamon

4 tbsp (19 g) freshly grated coconut or raw unsweetened coconut flakes

Vegetable oil, as needed

Powdered sugar, optional

Mix together the water, coconut milk, sugar and yeast in a large bowl. Allow the mixture to rest for 5 minutes. Add the egg and mix well until combined.

Add the flour, salt, cardamom seeds, nutmeg, cinnamon and coconut. Mix together until a dough forms.

Transfer the dough to a lightly floured work surface and knead until all of the ingredients are incorporated, about 5 minutes. The stickiness of the dough should almost be gone.

Place the dough in a greased bowl and cover it with a clean tea towel. Place the bowl in a warm spot and allow the dough to rise for 2 hours.

Divide the dough into 4 equal balls. Roll each ball flat and cut it into 6 triangles. Let these rest for 15 minutes.

Meanwhile, fill a large pot with 3 inches (8 cm) of oil and heat to 350°F (177°C).

Drop the dough into the oil gently. You will need to fry these in batches to avoid overcrowding the pot.

Fry the mandazi for 2 to 3 minutes per side, until golden brown.

Remove the mandazi from the oil using a slotted spoon and transfer them to a large baking sheet lined with paper towels.

Sprinkle the powdered sugar over the mandazi (if using).

NORTHERN AFRICA

North African cuisine is heavily influenced by regions around the Mediterranean Sea. The region is predominantly Muslim, and the staple foods are meat (beef, lamb and goat), as well as fruits, vegetables, dates and olives. You'll see a lot of overlap with Middle Eastern recipes in the ingredients that are found in this region like Shakshuka (page 110) or Moroccan-Spiced Veggie Couscous (page 125). I love the unique mix of African and Arab cultures due to Northern Africa's geographical placement.

HARISSA GRILLED CHICKEN

The first time I tasted harissa, I was blown away by the smoky depth of flavor. I knew I wanted to keep it in my refrigerator, so I started buying the store-bought version to season pretty much everything I was eating. The only problem was that a jar of harissa didn't last very long in my kitchen; so, I turned to making my own version at home. I added a can of fire-roasted tomatoes to my recipe to add some bulk to the sauce.

The smokiness of the harissa sauce really adds a lot of flavor to chicken that is being prepared on the grill. I love to grill harissa chicken in the summer. I'm instantly transported to memories of holidays like Memorial Day and Independence Day and large cookouts with family and friends.

MAKES 6 TO 8 SERVINGS

HARISSA SAUCE

2 large jarred or fresh roasted red bell peppers

5 cloves garlic

1 (15-oz [420-g]) can fire-roasted tomatoes, drained

2 tbsp (16 g) smoked paprika

2 medium jalapeño chiles

1 small habanero chile

6 tbsp (90 ml) olive oil

Ground cumin, to taste

Ground coriander, to taste

Crushed red pepper flakes, to taste

CHICKEN

1 tbsp (8 g) garlic powder

1 tbsp (8 g) paprika

½ tbsp (4 g) ground cumin

1 tsp ground cinnamon

1½ tsp (8 g) salt

1 tsp black pepper

5 lb (2.3 kg) chicken drumsticks

10 oz (300 ml) Harissa Sauce

To make the sauce, combine the bell peppers, garlic, tomatoes, smoked paprika, jalapeños, habanero, oil, cumin, coriander and crushed red pepper flakes in a food processor. Process until the mixture is uniform. Transfer the sauce to jars and store in the fridge for up to 2 weeks.

To make the chicken, preheat the grill to 400°F (204°C).

In a small bowl, combine the garlic powder, paprika, cumin, cinnamon, salt and black pepper.

Place the drumsticks and spice mixture in a large resealable bag. Shake the bag, ensuring that each piece of chicken is coated with the spices.

Place the drumsticks directly on the grill and flip them every 5 to 7 minutes.

Once the drumsticks start to brown, move them to the side of the grill, away from the direct heat. When the internal temperature of the drumsticks reaches 190°F (88°C), baste the chicken with the harissa sauce and cook for 2 to 5 minutes.

Remove the drumsticks from the grill and let them rest for 5 minutes before serving.

SHAKSHUKA
(SPICY TOMATO STEW WITH EGGS)

It makes me so happy whenever I see an African recipe break into the mainstream. Our food can often be left out, so to see other cultures celebrate and enjoy it brings a smile to my face. Shakshuka is very popular right now, and you can find so many variations and toppings for it. I wanted to take it back to tradition. No frills, no extras. Just the basics. It's spicy, thanks to the chiles and a good amount of smoked paprika, and the tomatoes bring a nice amount of acidity and sweetness.

MAKES 4 TO 6 SERVINGS

3 tbsp (45 ml) extra-virgin olive oil

1 medium onion, thinly sliced

1 large red bell pepper, thinly sliced

1 small habanero chile, thinly sliced

3 cloves garlic, minced

1½ tbsp (12 g) smoked paprika

1 tbsp (8 g) ground cumin

1 (28-oz [784-g]) can whole peeled tomatoes

Salt and black pepper, as needed

1 large bunch fresh cilantro, roughly chopped, divided

3 tbsp (10 g) fresh parsley, roughly chopped, divided

6 large eggs

Bread, for serving

Heat the oil in a large cast-iron skillet over high heat. Add the onion, bell pepper and habanero to the skillet and sauté for 10 minutes. Stir constantly to avoid burning the onion and bell pepper.

Add the garlic, smoked paprika and cumin and cook for 30 seconds, stirring constantly.

Add the tomatoes with their juices, breaking them into smaller pieces with a wooden spoon.

Reduce the heat to medium-low and simmer for 10 minutes. Season with the salt and black pepper and stir in half of the cilantro and 1½ tablespoons (5 g) of the parsley.

Using a wooden spoon, make a well near the edge of the skillet and break an egg directly into it. Using the spoon, cover the whites with a little sauce to hold them in place. Repeat this process with the remaining eggs.

Season the eggs with some salt, cover the skillet, reduce the heat to low and cook for 8 minutes. The egg whites should be set but the yolks still runny.

Sprinkle the remaining half of the cilantro and the remaining 1½ tablespoons (5 g) of parsley over the top. Serve with bread.

NORTH AFRICAN MEATBALLS

Every cook should have a go-to meatball recipe. They are perfect as an appetizer or as a dinner option on top of some rice or couscous. These meatballs are cooked in a spicy and sweet stew for an earthy and delicious flavor.

MAKES 4 TO 6 SERVINGS

MEATBALLS

1 lb (450 g) ground beef

2 slices stale white bread, crusts removed and torn into pieces

1 large egg

1 tsp ground cumin

1 tsp paprika

1 tsp ground cinnamon

½ tsp ground cardamom

1 tsp ground coriander

1 tsp salt

½ tsp black pepper

Olive oil, as needed

SAUCE

2 tbsp (30 ml) olive oil

1 clove garlic, minced

1 large onion, roughly chopped

2 tsp (6 g) minced fresh ginger

1 tsp ground cumin

1 tsp paprika

2 (2- to 4-inch [6- to 10-cm]) cinnamon sticks

1 tsp brown sugar

1 (14-oz [392-g]) can diced tomatoes

2 tbsp (19 g) dried currants

1 cup (240 ml) chicken stock

Salt and black pepper, as needed

To make the meatballs, combine the ground beef, bread, egg, cumin, paprika, cinnamon, cardamom, coriander, salt and black pepper in a large bowl. Make sure the mixture is well combined, then roll the meat into golf ball–size balls.

Heat the oil in a large skillet over medium-high heat. Brown the meatballs just until they have formed a dark crust on the bottom, about 6 minutes. Continue to brown the meatballs for 5 minutes, turning occasionally to brown all sides.

Transfer the meatballs to a plate and set it aside.

To make the sauce, heat the oil in the skillet. Add the garlic and sauté for 1 minute. Add the onion and sauté for 5 minutes.

Add the ginger, cumin, paprika, cinnamon sticks and brown sugar. Transfer the meatballs (along with any juices) back to the skillet. Toss the meatballs so that they are coated in the spices.

Add the tomatoes with their juices, currants and chicken stock. Season with salt and black pepper and stir to combine.

Reduce the heat to medium, cover the skillet and simmer for 20 minutes.

Serve with basmati rice or couscous. These can also be eaten on their own.

MOROCCAN-SPICED LAMB CHOPS

The first time I cooked lamb, I felt like such a grown-up. I was cooking a special dinner for my boyfriend's birthday, and I really wanted to impress him. I had never cooked lamb before and was somewhat intimidated, so I decided to pick up lamb chops rather than butchering the meat myself. Surprisingly, they were really easy to cook and the meal came out great! These lamb chops are flavored with spices from Morocco. The cumin and ginger go well with the lamb, and they help brighten that gamey flavor lamb can sometimes have. I love to serve these chops with a spiced veggie couscous. If you're new to cooking lamb, try cooking chops first.

MAKES 4 TO 6 SERVINGS

1 tsp ground cardamom

1 tsp ground cumin

½ tsp ground ginger

½ tsp ground cinnamon

¼ tsp black pepper

1 tsp salt

Olive oil, as needed

2 lb (900 g) lamb rib chops

3 cloves garlic, minced

Vegetable oil, as needed

½ cup fresh cilantro, roughly chopped

Couscous or rice, for serving

In a small bowl, combine the cardamom, cumin, ginger, cinnamon, black pepper and salt.

Drizzle some olive oil over the lamb chops. Pat the garlic all over the chops. Sprinkle the spice mixture over the chops, ensuring that they are evenly coated.

Heat some vegetable oil in a large skillet over high heat. Add the chops to the skillet and sear each side for 4 minutes, for a total of 8 minutes. The chops will be cooked to medium, or an internal temperature of 160°F (71°C).

Transfer the chops to a plate and garnish them with the cilantro. Serve with couscous or rice.

KOSHARI
(EGYPTIAN CASSEROLE)

This koshari is Egypt's national dish. I first had it at a Taste of Africa event and was amazed at all of the ingredients involved in this one dish. It's a starch lover's dream, packed with noodles, rice and lentils. It's so unique to have all of those ingredients in one dish, and they all complement each other so well. I like to think of this as a casserole.

MAKES 4 TO 6 SERVINGS

RICE, LENTILS AND MACARONI

2 tbsp (30 ml) olive oil

1 cup (211 g) basmati rice

2 cups (480 ml) vegetable stock

1 cup (201 g) brown lentils

2 cups (480 ml) water, plus more as needed

1 clove garlic

1 tsp ground cumin

1 bay leaf

2 tsp (10 g) salt

2 cups (232 g) elbow macaroni

SAUCE

2 tbsp (30 ml) olive oil

1 large onion, finely chopped

2 cloves garlic, minced

1 (16-oz [448-g]) can diced tomatoes

2 tsp (2 g) Ras El Hanout (page 129)

Salt and black pepper, to taste

¼ tsp crushed red pepper flakes

1 tbsp (15 ml) red wine vinegar

CRISPY ONION TOPPING

Vegetable oil, as needed

2 large onions, thinly sliced

1 (15-oz [420-g]) can chickpeas, drained and rinsed

To make the rice, lentils and macaroni, heat the olive oil in a large saucepan over medium heat. Add the rice to the saucepan, toasting it for 2 to 3 minutes. Pour the vegetable stock onto the rice and bring it to a boil.

Once the rice is boiling, reduce the heat to low, cover the saucepan and simmer the rice for 15 to 20 minutes, until it is cooked.

While the rice is cooking, rinse the lentils. Place the lentils and water in a small pot over medium heat. Add the garlic, cumin, bay leaf and salt and bring to a boil. Once the lentils are boiling, reduce the heat to low, cover the pot and simmer for 30 to 40 minutes. The lentils should be tender, and all of the liquid should have evaporated.

Bring a medium pot of water to a boil over high heat. Add the macaroni and cook until it is al dente, 7 to 8 minutes.

To make the sauce, heat the olive oil in a large saucepan over medium-high heat. Add the onion and sauté until it is soft and translucent, about 5 minutes. Add the garlic and cook for 30 seconds.

Add the tomatoes with their juices, ras el hanout, salt and black pepper and crushed red pepper flakes. Stir the ingredients together, then add the vinegar. Bring the sauce to a simmer, cover and cook for 20 minutes, stirring occasionally.

Meanwhile, to make the crispy onion topping, heat some oil in a medium pot over high heat. Add the onion slices and fry until they are golden brown in color, about 5 minutes. Remove them from the oil using a slotted spoon and place them on a paper towel to drain.

Add the rice, lentils and macaroni to a large bowl. Toss together until they are mixed well.

Pour the sauce into the bowl and mix the ingredients together.

Top the koshari with the crispy onions and chickpeas.

LEBLEBI
(NORTH AFRICAN CHICKPEA SOUP)

This is one of my favorite African soups. Chickpeas are great for a hearty meal because they absorb flavors and spices so well. There's just so much flavor in this recipe—and when you combine this with a warm, chewy flatbread and smoky Harissa Sauce (page 109), it's a seriously delicious meal!

MAKES 4 TO 6 SERVINGS

4 tbsp (60 ml) olive oil

1 large white onion, diced

3 tsp (8 g) cumin seeds

2 tsp (6 g) smoked paprika

2 tsp (2 g) crushed red pepper flakes

½ cup (20 g) fresh cilantro, roughly chopped

2 cloves garlic, minced

1 cup (161 g) crushed tomatoes

3 (16-oz [448-g]) cans chickpeas, drained and rinsed

Water, as needed

2 tbsp (30 g) salt

Aish Baladi (page 130), for serving

Harissa Sauce (page 109), for serving

Heat the oil in a large pot over medium-high heat. Add the onion and sauté until it is soft and translucent, 5 to 6 minutes.

Add the cumin seeds, smoked paprika, crushed red pepper flakes, cilantro and garlic. Stir the ingredients together and cook for 1 minute. Add the tomatoes and cook, stirring frequently, for 5 minutes.

Add the chickpeas, followed by enough water to cover them. Bring the soup to a boil.

Once the soup is boiling, reduce the heat to low, cover the pot and simmer for 20 minutes.

Using an immersion blender, partially blend the chickpeas. You want to have some whole chickpeas. Alternatively, you can transfer 1 to 2 ladles of the chickpeas to a blender, blend them and return them to the soup.

Season the soup with the salt. Stir the chickpea puree into the soup and ladle the soup into individual bowls. Serve with Aish Baladi and Harissa Sauce.

MOROCCAN CHICKEN TAGINE

I never get tired of eating chicken. There are so many variations that the possibilities are endless when it comes to combinations. This Moroccan chicken is special because it's made in a tagine, a vessel used in Northern Africa to cook stews and meat. It's essentially a clay pot and imparts a lot of flavor into whatever is cooking inside it.

MAKES 4 TO 6 SERVINGS

1 large onion, roughly chopped

3 medium carrots, diced

2 large Roma tomatoes, roughly chopped

3 cloves garlic, minced

2½ lb (1 kg) chicken (any cut), cut into 1-inch (3-cm) pieces

1 tsp curry powder

2 tbsp (16 g) chili powder

1 tsp ground coriander

3 tbsp (9 g) roughly chopped fresh parsley

2 tbsp (30 ml) olive oil

1 cup (240 ml) water

1 lb (450 g) Yukon gold potatoes, peeled and cut into ½-inch (6-mm) thick slices

¼ cup (38 g) frozen peas

Place the onion, carrots, tomatoes and garlic in the bottom of the tagine.

Place the chicken on top of the vegetables. Sprinkle the curry powder, chili powder, coriander and parsley over the chicken. Add the oil and water.

Cover the tagine and cook over medium heat for 1 hour.

After 1 hour, add the potatoes on top of the chicken. Cover the tagine and cook for 20 minutes, until the potatoes have softened. Add the peas and cook for 5 minutes.

Serve immediately with rice or couscous.

ONE-POT NORTH AFRICAN CHICKEN AND RICE

The first time I ever made chicken and rice in one pot was amazing. The flavor and juices from the chicken seeped down into the rice and gave it an incredible flavor. Everything in the pot was seasoned, and it turned out to be a treat. This chicken and rice is just like that. Both the rice and the chicken are seasoned with flavors most popular in North Africa, and they finish cooking together in the oven. It's absolutely delicious.

MAKES 4 TO 6 SERVINGS

CHICKEN

5 skin-on, bone-in chicken thighs

2 tbsp (30 ml) fresh lemon juice

2 tbsp (16 g) ground turmeric

1 tbsp (8 g) ground cumin

½ tbsp (4 g) ground coriander

1 tbsp (3 g) dried oregano

4 cloves garlic, minced

1 tsp salt

1 tsp black pepper

RICE

2 tbsp (30 ml) olive oil, divided

1 small onion, finely chopped

1 tbsp (3 g) dried oregano

1 tbsp (8 g) ground turmeric

1 tsp ground cumin

1 clove garlic, minced

1½ cups (317 g) basmati rice

1½ cups (360 ml) chicken stock

1 cup (240 ml) water

1 tsp salt

Grilled lemon slices and fresh parsley, for garnishing

To make the chicken, combine the chicken thighs, lemon juice, turmeric, cumin, coriander, oregano, garlic, salt and black pepper in a large resealable bag. Let the chicken marinate for at least 30 minutes in the refrigerator (preferably overnight for more flavor).

Preheat the oven to 375°F (191°C).

To make the rice, heat 1 tablespoon (15 ml) of the oil in a large ovenproof skillet over medium-high heat. Place the chicken in the skillet skin-side down and cook until it is golden brown, 3 to 5 minutes. Then flip the chicken over and cook the other side until golden brown, 3 to 5 minutes.

Remove the chicken and set it aside.

Remove any black or burned bits from the skillet, then add the remaining 1 tablespoon (15 ml) of oil.

Add the onion, oregano, turmeric and cumin. Sauté until the onion becomes translucent, 2 to 3 minutes.

Add the garlic and rice and sauté for 1 minute, just until the rice begins to turn golden.

Add the chicken stock, water and salt and bring the mixture to a simmer. Place the cooked chicken thighs directly on top of the rice. Cover the skillet with a lid and transfer it to the oven.

Bake the chicken and rice in the oven for 30 minutes. After 30 minutes, remove the skillet's lid and bake for 15 minutes, until all the liquid has been absorbed.

Remove the skillet from the oven and let it sit for 10 minutes before serving. Garnish with the grilled lemon slices and fresh parsley.

MOROCCAN-SPICED VEGGIE COUSCOUS

Spice is the name of the game for this couscous. I find that couscous, unless seasoned well, can be quite bland. I've added a lot of seasoning to the veggies and couscous because I want it to be bold and "in your face." One bite of this, and you're instantly transported to the bustling streets of Morocco.

MAKES 4 TO 6 SERVINGS

2 tbsp (30 ml) olive oil

1 medium red onion, finely chopped

1 large yellow bell pepper, finely chopped

1 medium orange bell pepper, finely chopped

1 large zucchini, finely chopped

3 cloves garlic, minced

1 cup (240 ml) chicken or vegetable stock

2 cups (300 g) frozen peas

1 tsp paprika

1 tsp ground cumin

1 tsp ground coriander

½ tsp ground turmeric

½ tsp ground cinnamon

1½ cups (270 g) dry couscous

1 (16-oz [448-g]) can chickpeas, drained and rinsed

½ cup (50 g) dried cranberries

Zest and juice of 2 lemons

1 pint (161 g) cherry tomatoes, cut in half

2 tbsp (6 g) fresh cilantro, minced

2 tsp (2 g) fresh parsley, minced

Salt and black pepper, to taste

Heat the oil in a medium skillet over medium heat.

Add the onion, yellow bell pepper, orange bell pepper and zucchini and sauté for 10 minutes, just until they begin to soften.

Add the garlic and sauté for 2 minutes.

Turn off the heat, and set the skillet aside.

In a medium saucepan, bring the chicken stock to a boil over high heat. Add the peas, paprika, cumin, coriander, turmeric and cinnamon and cook for 2 minutes. Add the couscous, chickpeas and cranberries and stir.

Remove the saucepan from the heat, cover and let it stand for 5 minutes, until the liquid is absorbed.

Add the vegetable mixture, lemon zest and juice, tomatoes, cilantro and parsley and toss until the ingredients are mixed well. Season with the salt and black pepper. Fluff with a fork.

Serve either warm or cold.

MAAQUODA
(POTATO FRITTERS)

Potato fritters are there for you to nibble on whenever you need a snack. These fritters are commonly made during the months of Ramadan and are a huge hit in Northern Africa. I've kept them vegetarian, but you can add any type of meat or seafood if you'd like.

MAKES 6 TO 8 SERVINGS

2 lb (900 g) Yukon gold potatoes, peeled and cut into large chunks

Salt and black pepper, as needed

¼ cup (30 g) panko breadcrumbs

1 tsp garlic powder

1 tsp ground turmeric

1 tsp ground cumin

1 tsp onion powder

3 tbsp (9 g) fresh parsley, finely chopped

2 large eggs, beaten

Vegetable oil, as needed

All-purpose flour, as needed

Place the potatoes in a large pot. Cover them with cold water and bring them to a boil over high heat. Season the potatoes with salt and cook for 30 minutes, until the potatoes are tender.

Drain the potatoes and transfer them to a large bowl. Mash the potatoes with a wooden spoon. Add the breadcrumbs, garlic powder, turmeric, cumin, onion powder, parsley and eggs. Season the mixture with salt and black pepper and stir to combine.

Shape the potato mixture into patties 2 to 3 inches (6 to 8 cm) in diameter.

Heat some oil in a large pot until it reaches 350°F (177°C). Place the flour in a shallow dish.

Coat the patties in flour, covering both sides. Shake to remove any excess flour. Fry the patties in the oil until they are golden brown, about 3 minutes per side.

Remove the fritters from the oil and place them on a paper towel to drain. Repeat this process with the remaining patties.

NORTH AFRICAN POTATO SALAD WITH RAS EL HANOUT

While diving into North African recipes, I found that a lot of them called for a seasoning called ras el hanout. Such a spice was not easily found, so I asked my neighbor for her recipe. She didn't have an exact recipe, but over time, I managed to get the ingredients from her, and this is a recipe that we came up with together. She advised how much of each spice should be used to make the perfect blend.

This blend isn't spicy. It boasts more of an earthy and pungent taste and is perfect as a marinade or spice rub. I also love to use it to season vegetables and sides like potato salad—I grew tired of traditional potato salad recipes, so I decided to take the flavors and inspiration of Northern Africa by replacing the mayo with Greek yogurt and adding ras el hanout.

MAKES 4 TO 6 SERVINGS

RAS EL HANOUT

1½ tsp (4 g) coriander seeds

1 tsp cumin seeds

1 tsp crushed red pepper flakes

1 tsp paprika

1 tsp ground cinnamon

½ tsp ground cardamom

½ tsp ground ginger

½ tsp ground turmeric

POTATO SALAD

2 lb (900 g) Yukon gold potatoes, peeled and cut into 1-inch (3-cm) cubes

Salt, as needed

3 tbsp (45 ml) olive oil

1½ tbsp (12 g) Ras el Hanout

¾ cup (184 g) Greek yogurt

2 tbsp (30 ml) sherry vinegar

½ cup (20 g) fresh mint, roughly chopped

½ cup (20 g) fresh parsley, roughly chopped

Zest and juice of 1 lemon

To make the ras el hanout, toast the coriander and cumin seeds in a small skillet over medium heat. Stir the seeds every now and then, until they are dark in color, about 5 minutes. Remove the skillet from the heat and allow the seeds to cool.

Add the toasted seeds to a spice grinder along with the crushed red pepper flakes and process until they are finely ground. Transfer the mixture to a small bowl.

Add the paprika, cinnamon, cardamom, ginger and turmeric to the bowl and mix the spices together. Store the ras el hanout in an airtight container.

To make the potato salad, place the potatoes in a large pot and cover them completely with cold water. Add salt. Bring the potatoes to a boil over high heat, reduce the heat to medium-low and simmer the potatoes until they are tender but not mushy, 8 to 10 minutes. Drain the potatoes and transfer them to a large bowl. Set them aside to cool.

Heat the oil in a small skillet over medium heat. Add the ras el hanout and cook just until the spices start to smell fragrant, 1 to 2 minutes. Set the skillet aside.

Once the potatoes are cool, pour the ras el hanout–infused oil all over the potatoes. Stir well. Then add the yogurt, vinegar, mint, parsley and lemon zest and juice. Mix well to combine.

Taste and adjust the seasonings. Chill the potato salad in the fridge at least 1 hour before serving (ideally, allow it to chill for 4 hours).

AISH BALADI
(EGYPTIAN FLATBREAD)

This will be an accompaniment to all your North African soups and stews. It's simple, delicious and foolproof. I've been known to eat pretty much the entire batch myself. That's how good these are.

MAKES 4 TO 6 SERVINGS

2 cups (250 g) all-purpose flour
1 tsp salt
¾ cup (180 ml) milk
1 tbsp (15 ml) olive oil

Preheat the oven to 375°F (191°C). Line a large baking sheet with aluminum foil.

Whisk the flour and salt together in a large bowl.

Gradually add the milk and oil and mix together until a dough forms.

Transfer the dough to a lightly floured work surface. Knead for 15 minutes, until the dough is smooth and stretchy. Cover the dough with a tea towel and allow it to rest for 15 to 30 minutes.

Divide the dough into 4 equal balls. Roll out each ball to ¼ inch (6 mm) thick.

Place the dough on the baking sheet and bake until it is light brown, 8 to 10 minutes. Eat right away.

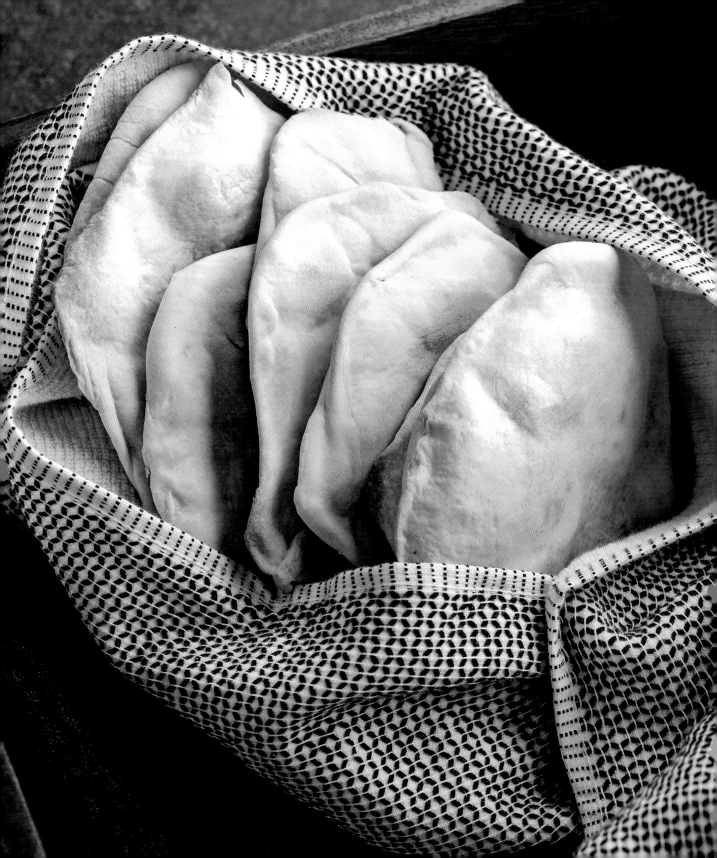

CHARMOULA EGGPLANT

I never cared for eggplant until I had it seasoned with this charmoula sauce. It's spicy and aromatic and, surprisingly, reminds me of meat. Serve this with couscous or rice.

MAKES 4 SERVINGS

2 cloves garlic, minced
2 tsp (6 g) ground cumin
2 tsp (6 g) ground coriander
¾ tsp ground cinnamon
1 tsp crushed red pepper flakes
1 tsp smoked paprika
¼ cup (60 ml) olive oil
2 tsp (10 g) salt
2 medium eggplants
Rice or couscous, for serving

Preheat the oven to 400°F (204°C). Line a medium baking sheet with aluminum foil.

In a small bowl, combine the garlic, cumin, coriander, cinnamon, crushed red pepper flakes and paprika. Add the oil and salt and mix the ingredients together. Set the charmoula sauce aside.

Cut the eggplants in half lengthwise. With a knife, score the flesh of each slice with diagonal cuts to form hash marks. You want to cut deep, but be careful to not cut all the way through to the other side of the eggplants.

Place the eggplants on the baking sheet, scored-side up.

Spoon the charmoula sauce over the eggplants, spreading it evenly.

Bake the eggplants in the oven for 45 minutes, until they are soft.

Serve over rice or couscous.

SOUTHERN AFRICA

Southern Africa is another region of Africa with heavy influences from all around the world. Due to intensive periods of colonialism from the Germans, French, Italians, Greeks and Portuguese, South African food is often referred to as "rainbow" cuisine. Curries, lemons and chiles are popular ingredients that are used often, and there are also indigenous flavors and recipes that largely influence the cuisine. To me, South African cuisine is a melting pot of amazing flavors—and that is what I love most about it.

CHICKEN WITH FIERY PERI PERI SAUCE

Spicy sauces and condiments may be what I love most about African cooking. This sauce is complex in taste, with notes of acidity, heat and sweetness; and this sauce is so versatile it can be used on almost anything. I love to marinate chicken and shrimp in it before grilling, and it also makes a great dipping sauce. You'll find many versions of this sauce, but what takes it over the top for me is the addition of fresh lemon juice and extra-virgin olive oil. The heat of the peri peri sauce goes so well with the chicken. It's a sweet, tangy, spicy explosion of flavor and the chicken soaks it up perfectly. This is like Nando's, a popular chicken restaurant in the UK known for making Peri Peri chicken, but homemade and a million times better.

MAKES 6 TO 8 SERVINGS

PERI PERI SAUCE

2 large red bell peppers, chargrilled

1 large red onion, char-grilled

1 cup (170 g) African bird's eye chiles or 8 red Thai chiles and 2 small habanero chiles

4 cloves garlic

¾ cup (180 ml) fresh lemon juice, divided

½ cup (120 ml) apple cider vinegar, divided

Zest of 2 lemons, divided

1 tbsp (8 g) smoked paprika

1½ tsp (2 g) dried oregano

2 bay leaves

Salt and black pepper, to taste

½ cup (120 ml) extra-virgin olive oil

CHICKEN

2½ to 3 lb (1.1 to 1.4 kg) bone-in or boneless chicken (any cut)

2 tsp (10 g) salt

2 tsp (6 g) black pepper

2 tsp (6 g) garlic powder

1 to 2 cups (240 to 480 ml) Peri Peri Sauce

To make the sauce, combine the bell peppers, onion, African bird's eye chiles, garlic, ½ cup (120 ml) of the lemon juice, ¼ cup (60 ml) of the vinegar, zest of 1 lemon, smoked paprika and oregano in a food processor. Process the ingredients until the mixture is completely smooth.

Transfer the sauce to a medium-size saucepan over medium heat and add the bay leaves and salt and black pepper. Simmer for 30 minutes, stirring occasionally. Remove the sauce from the heat, remove the bay leaves and allow the sauce to cool completely.

Once the sauce has cooled, transfer it back to the food processor and add the zest of the remaining lemon, the remaining ¼ cup (60 ml) of lemon juice and the remaining ¼ cup (60 ml) of vinegar. Blend the sauce for a few minutes while streaming in the oil slowly.

The sauce is finished and ready to be used as a marinade on any protein of your choice or as a condiment. Leftover sauce can be refrigerated for up to 1 week.

To make the chicken, place the chicken in a large resealable bag. Add the salt, black pepper, garlic powder and Peri Peri Sauce. Seal the bag and toss the chicken so that it is evenly coated with the marinade. Place it in the fridge and let the chicken marinate for 24 hours.

Preheat the grill to medium heat. Remove the chicken from the bag, shaking off any excess marinade. Place the chicken on the grill. Grill the chicken for 10 to 15 minutes per side, or until it is fully cooked and has an internal temperature of 165°F (74°C). Brush any extra sauce on the chicken during the last 5 minutes of cooking.

Serve immediately with extra dipping sauce at the table and with your choice of sides (white rice, french fries, corn and so on).

PRAWN NACIONAL
(MOZAMBIQUE PRAWNS)

Hands down, this is the best prawn recipe I have ever tasted. It's spicy, tangy, sweet and tastes very similar to Peri Peri Sauce (page 137), except instead of a sauce, it's an oil. It's wildly addicting and irresistible. Just one prawn will have you coming back for more. Note that you will need to make the oil at least one day in advance of cooking the prawns.

MAKES 6 TO 8 SERVINGS

8 African bird's eye chiles or 8 small habanero chiles

1½ cups (360 ml) vegetable oil

4 tbsp (60 ml) fresh lemon juice

2 tbsp (18 g) crushed garlic

1 tsp salt

1 tsp smoked paprika

4 lb (1.8 kg) large prawns or shrimp

At least 24 hours in advance of cooking the prawns, roughly chop the bird's eye chiles. (If you are concerned about the heat, you can remove the seeds or adjust the number of chiles to your liking.)

Heat the oil in a large skillet over medium heat. Take care that you do not let the oil come to a boil.

Add the lemon juice, garlic, salt, smoked paprika and chiles to the oil.

Remove the skillet from the heat, and transfer the oil to a clean jar or bottle. Steep the oil for 1 day or more if you like. The oil will begin to turn a deep red color.

Wash and clean the prawns by deveining them. To devein the prawns, make a shallow slit down the middle of their backs. The black veins should be visible. Lift out the black veins with the tip of your knife and discard them. (Do not remove the shells.) Spread the two sides of the prawns apart slightly. Set them aside.

Add the prawns to a large bowl, and pour the oil over the prawns. Stir to combine. Cover the bowl with plastic wrap and let the prawns marinate in the fridge for 2 hours.

Preheat the oven to 350°F (177°C).

Transfer the prawns to a large baking sheet and bake just until they start to turn pink, 7 to 8 minutes.

Use a slotted spoon to remove the prawns from the baking sheet, and place them on a plate lined with paper towels.

Serve immediately.

SOUTH AFRICAN YELLOW RICE

Heat and sweetness is one of my favorite flavor combinations. Just when you feel like a dish is too hot, you get an underlying layer of sweetness that brings it back down. That's how this yellow rice is: it's fragrant and delicious!

MAKES 6 TO 8 SERVINGS

3 tbsp (42 g) unsalted butter
1 tbsp (9 g) brown sugar
1½ tsp (5 g) ground turmeric
½ tsp hot curry powder
2 cups (422 g) jasmine rice
4 cups (960 ml) chicken stock
½ cup (76 g) raisins

Heat the butter in a large pot over medium-high heat.

Add the brown sugar, turmeric and curry powder and cook for 1 to 2 minutes.

Add the rice, stirring to coat it with the seasonings. Toast the rice for 1 to 2 minutes.

Add the chicken stock to the pot and bring the mixture to a boil. Reduce the heat to medium-low, add the raisins and cover the pot. Simmer for 20 minutes, until the rice is cooked through.

Fluff the rice with a fork before serving.

THE GATSBY

This is such a fun recipe because of the story behind it. This monstrous sandwich creation was invented in Cape Town, South Africa, by a local fish and chips shop that had to feed a hungry group of laborers but had run out of fish. The solution? Fill a sandwich with french fries and bologna. The laborers loved it and it has remained a very popular street food. Now, if you're wondering why it's called The Gatsby, a movie based on *The Great Gatsby* happened to be screening at the time the sandwich was created. How cool is that?

MAKES 2 SERVINGS

1 tsp olive oil

4 slices bologna

Ketchup, to taste

Peri Peri Sauce (page 137), to taste

1 crusty hoagie roll, split in half and lightly toasted

Freshly cooked French fries, as needed

½ cup (40 g) shredded lettuce

Heat the oil in a large skillet over medium-high heat. Add the bologna and cook until it is browned on both sides, 2 to 3 minutes per side.

In a small bowl, mix together the ketchup and Peri Peri Sauce.

Arrange the bologna slices on the bottom half of the hoagie roll. Place French fries on top of the meat, followed by the shredded lettuce.

Spread the ketchup mixture on the other half of the hoagie roll.

Close the sandwich and serve immediately.

KOTA
(BUNNY CHOW)

Bunny Chow reminds me of curry from India. It's warming, comforting and a stick-to-your-ribs kind of meal. Make sure you grab a good loaf of bread to serve as a bowl for this chow. The insides will be perfect for dipping into!

MAKES 4 TO 6 SERVINGS

½ cup (120 ml) canola oil

1 medium onion, diced

2 tsp (6 g) minced garlic

1 tsp minced fresh ginger

1 (2- to 4-inch [6- to 10-cm]) cinnamon stick

1 tsp paprika

2 cardamom pods

3 tbsp (24 g) curry powder

Salt, as needed

2 medium tomatoes, diced

1 lb (450 g) boneless, skinless chicken breast, cut into bite-size pieces

1½ cups (360 ml) chicken stock

2 medium Yukon gold potatoes, peeled and cut into ½- to 1-inch (13-mm to 3-cm]) cubes

1 (15-oz [420-g]) can chickpeas, drained and rinsed

4 to 6 bread bowls, for serving

Heat the oil in a large saucepan over high heat. Add the onion, garlic, ginger, cinnamon stick, paprika, cardamom pods, curry powder and salt. Cook for 3 minutes, stirring constantly to prevent the mixture from burning.

Add the tomatoes and chicken to the saucepan. Sauté for 5 minutes.

Add the chicken stock, potatoes and chickpeas. Bring the mixture to a boil, reduce the heat to medium-low and let the kota simmer for 25 minutes, until it thickens.

Transfer the kota to hollowed-out bread bowls of your choice.

CALULU DE PEIXE
(ANGOLAN FISH STEW)

This stew reminds me of the kind of stew my mum loves to eat. She loves fresh fish and will devour it in a stew. I like this stew because it's light—it's definitely filling, but won't leave you feeling like you've overeaten.

MAKES 4 TO 6 SERVINGS

1 lb (450 g) halibut, cut into 2-inch (6-cm) pieces

2 tbsp (30 ml) fresh lemon juice

3 cloves garlic, minced

1 tsp salt

1 tsp black pepper

1 tbsp (15 ml) vegetable oil

2 medium white onions, diced

4 medium tomatoes, diced

2 medium jalapeño chiles or serrano chiles, diced

¾ cup (75 g) okra, trimmed and cut into ¼-inch (6-mm) rounds

2 bay leaves

¼ cup (60 ml) palm oil

1½ cups (360 ml) vegetable stock

1 cup (30 g) tightly packed spinach, roughly chopped

Place the halibut in a large bowl. Add the lemon juice, garlic, salt and black pepper. Mix the ingredients together and let the fish marinate for 10 minutes.

Heat the vegetable oil in a large pot over medium-high heat. Add the onions and cook for 2 to 3 minutes, until they are translucent.

Reduce the heat to medium and add the fish to the pot.

Add the tomatoes, jalapeños, okra, bay leaves, palm oil and vegetable stock to the pot. Do not stir, as you don't want to break up the fish.

Cover the pot and cook for 20 minutes.

Add the spinach and stir gently. Cover the pot and simmer for 5 minutes. Serve.

DOVI

(ZIMBABWEAN PEANUT STEW)

My vegan and vegetarian friends: You didn't think I'd leave you guys hanging, did you? This peanut stew is filled with veggies and has a delicious kick of heat to it. A lot of African recipes can be made vegan or vegetarian. All you need to do is leave the meat out and replace it with veggies!

MAKES 4 TO 6 SERVINGS

2 tbsp (30 ml) olive oil

2 medium onions, roughly chopped

2 medium serrano chiles, diced

4 cloves garlic, minced

4 cups (960 ml) vegetable stock, divided

3 tbsp (45 ml) Peri Peri Sauce (page 137)

1½ cups (270 g) peanut butter

2 tbsp (20 g) tomato paste

1 tsp cayenne pepper

2 medium carrots, roughly chopped

1 cup (99 g) okra, whole

2 cups (60 g) tightly packed spinach

Salt, to taste

Heat the oil in a large pot over medium-high heat. Add the onions, serrano chiles and garlic. Sauté for 2 to 3 minutes.

Add 1 cup (240 ml) of the vegetable stock, Peri Peri Sauce and peanut butter. Using a whisk, vigorously stir the mixture until the peanut butter has dissolved.

Add the remaining 3 cups (720 ml) of vegetable stock, tomato paste, cayenne and carrots. Reduce the heat to medium-low, cover the pot and let the stew simmer for 10 minutes.

Add the okra. Stir the stew and cover the pot. Simmer for 10 minutes.

Add the spinach and salt to the pot, mixing well. Cover the pot and cook for 2 minutes, until the spinach has wilted and reduced in size.

VETKOEK
(FAT CAKE)

Fat cakes are another popular street food of South Africa. They look exactly like their name: f at cakes that are stuffed with curry beef filling. Think of them like a meat pie or samosa, just with a sweeter dough.

MAKES 6 TO 8 SERVINGS

CURRY BEEF

2 tbsp (30 ml) vegetable oil

1 large onion, diced

2 cloves garlic, minced

1 tsp ground ginger

1 tbsp (8 g) curry powder

1 tsp paprika

2 medium tomatoes, finely chopped

2 cups (450 g) diced Yukon gold potatoes

1 lb (450 g) ground beef

Salt, as needed

1 cup (150 g) frozen peas and carrots, thawed

CAKE

1 tsp salt

3 tbsp (36 g) sugar

2 cups (480 ml) lukewarm water

1 (¼-oz [7-g]) packet active dry yeast

4 cups (360 g) cake flour

Vegetable oil, as needed

To make the curry beef, heat the oil in a large skillet over high heat. Add the onion, garlic, ginger, curry powder and paprika and sauté for 3 minutes, stirring constantly to prevent the mixture from burning.

Next, add the tomatoes, potatoes, ground beef and salt. Cook for 10 minutes, until the meat is brown.

Add the peas and carrots and cook for 2 minutes. Remove the skillet from the heat and allow the curry beef to cool completely.

To make the cake, combine the salt, sugar, water and yeast in a large bowl. Allow the mixture to rest for 5 minutes. Add the flour to the bowl and mix the ingredients together until a dough forms.

Cover the bowl with a tea towel and allow the dough to rise in a warm spot for 2 hours.

Transfer the dough to a floured work surface. Knead for 5 minutes.

Roll out the dough until it is about 1 inch (3 cm) thick. Use a cookie cutter or the lid from a jar to cut out round shapes.

Heat the oil to 350°F (177°C) in a large pot. Once the oil is hot, fry the cakes until they are golden brown, 3 to 5 minutes. Remove the cakes from the oil and transfer them to a plate lined with paper towels to drain.

Split the cakes in half with a knife and fill them with some of the curry beef.

BOBOTIE
(SOUTH AFRICAN MEAT PIE)

I loved meatloaf as a child. Seasoned beef with delicious ketchup on top was my absolute favorite. I like to call this bobotie the "adult meatloaf." It's packed with seasonings and topped with a crunchy yet moist topping that is so satisfying.

MAKES 6 TO 8 SERVINGS

3 slices white bread

1½ cups (360 ml) milk, divided

2 tbsp (30 ml) olive oil

2 large onions, roughly chopped

1 tbsp (8 g) curry powder

1 tsp dried oregano

1 tsp ground cumin

1 tsp ground turmeric

2 cloves garlic, minced

1 lb (450 g) ground beef

¼ cup (80 g) mango chutney

1 tbsp (20 g) apricot jam

Zest and juice of 1 lemon

1 tsp tomato paste

Salt and black pepper, as needed

2 large eggs

2 bay leaves

Preheat the oven to 350°F (177°C).

In a medium bowl, soak the bread in 1 cup (240 ml) of the milk. Set aside.

Heat the oil in a large ovenproof skillet over medium heat. Add the onions and cook 2 to 3 minutes, until the onions are soft.

Add the curry powder, oregano, cumin, turmeric and garlic. Stir and cook for 2 minutes.

Next, add the ground beef, breaking it into pieces with a wooden spoon. Cook the beef 7 to 10 minutes, until it has browned. Once the beef has browned, turn off the heat. Add the chutney, apricot jam, lemon zest, lemon juice and tomato paste. Season the mixture with the salt and black pepper.

Squeeze the milk from the bread, reserving the soaking milk. Tear the bread into pieces and add them to the beef mixture.

Add the remaining ½ cup (120 ml) of milk to the soaking milk. Add the eggs to the milk and whisk them together. Season the mixture with salt and black pepper.

Pour the milk mixture over the meat. Place the bay leaves on top.

Bake the bobotie, uncovered, for 30 to 40 minutes, until it is golden brown.

BRAAIBROODJIE
(SOUTH AFRICAN GRILLED CHEESE)

I used to be a barista in my university's library. We also had a deli attached to our coffee shop, and I would sometimes help out there. On the menu was a grilled cheese and tomato sandwich, and I loved it. This South African grilled cheese is better, though, because of the sweet mango chutney and flavors of onion and tomatoes.

MAKES 4 TO 6 SERVINGS

1 to 2 tbsp (15 to 30 ml) vegetable oil

3 medium onions, thinly sliced

4 large tomatoes, thinly sliced

½ tsp minced garlic

Salt and black pepper, to taste

Butter, as needed

8 slices white bread

8 slices Gruyère cheese

1 (12-oz [336-g]) jar mango chutney

Heat the oil in a large skillet over medium heat. Add the onions, tomatoes, garlic and salt and black pepper and sauté for 5 minutes. Remove the skillet from the heat and set it aside.

Butter each slice of the bread on both sides. On 4 slices of bread, place a slice of Gruyère. Top the Gruyère with a spoonful of the tomato mixture, followed by a spoonful of mango chutney, followed by another slice of Gruyère. Place the remaining 4 slices of bread on top.

Heat some butter in a large skillet over medium heat. Add a sandwich to the skillet and cook 3 minutes per side, or until it is golden brown and the cheese has melted. Repeat the process with the remaining sandwiches.

ZANZIBAR PIZZA

This is my take on a unique but popular street food in Zanzibar. How or where it was originated is unknown, but if you visit the Forodhani Gardens in Stone Town, Zanzibar, you'll find it being made there with processed cheese and mayo. I opted to leave those ingredients out. This is a lighter, healthier version.

MAKES 2 TO 4 SERVINGS

2 cups (250 g) all-purpose flour

½ tsp salt, plus more as needed

½ cup (120 ml) water

1 cup (240 ml) vegetable oil, plus more as needed

1 lb (450 g) ground beef

Black pepper, as needed

2 cloves garlic, minced

½ tsp finely chopped fresh ginger

3 small serrano chiles, diced

½ medium red onion, finely chopped

6 large eggs

Sift the flour into a large bowl. Add the ½ teaspoon of salt and the water and mix to make a smooth dough. Knead the dough for 5 minutes.

Divide the dough into 6 equal balls. Pour the oil over the balls, making sure they are coated well. Cover the dough balls with a tea towel and let them rest for 2 hours.

Heat a large skillet over medium-high heat. Add the ground beef, salt, black pepper, garlic and ginger. Break up the beef with a wooden spoon and stir, ensuring that all the seasonings are mixed in. Add the serrano chiles and onion and cook until the meat is brown, 10 to 15 minutes.

Roll a dough ball flat into a very thin circle about 10 inches (25 cm) in diameter. Add a spoonful of the beef mixture on top of the dough. Add an egg to the top of the meat. Fold all 4 edges of the dough inward, like you're making an envelope. Press the edges down to seal them. Repeat this process with the remaining dough balls and filling.

Heat some oil in a large skillet. Place the dough packets in the skillet and cook on each side for 5 to 8 minutes, until they are golden brown and the eggs are cooked.

Cut each pizza into 4 squares.

SWEET POTATO FRITTERS

If you want to do something different with your sweet potatoes, try your hand at these fritters. There is a hint of sweetness, but they are more on the savory side. I love to have these as a side dish to grilled fish or chicken—they're a nice switch from rice or couscous. To get them extra crispy, make sure you squeeze out all the water in the sweet potato. The best way to do this is with a tea towel.

MAKES 6 TO 8 SERVINGS

1 lb (450 g) sweet potatoes, peeled

Boiling water, as needed

1 cup (125 g) all-purpose flour

1 large egg

¼ cup (58 g) butter, melted

Pinch of salt

Vegetable oil, as needed

Grate the potatoes with a box grater. Place the potatoes in a large heatproof bowl and cover them with boiling water. Let the potatoes stand for 20 minutes.

Drain the potatoes well, squeezing out any excess water. Transfer the potatoes to another large bowl.

Combine the potatoes with the flour, egg, butter and salt. Add a little water to the mixture if you find that it is too stiff.

Heat the oil to 375°F (191°C) in a large pot. Once the oil has heated, carefully drop the sweet potato batter into the oil a spoonful at a time. Fry for 3 to 5 minutes, until the fritters are golden brown.

Remove the fritters from the oil with a slotted spoon and place them on a paper towel to drain. Serve the fritters hot.

MALVA PUDDING

Desserts are not my forte. I usually mess them up somehow. This malva pudding is the one exception to my dessert struggles. My first time making it turned out perfectly. I immediately knew that if I managed to make this without any issue, it was a recipe I had to share. It has a spongy carmelized texture and tastes like a sweet pudding. The addition of apricot jam sweetens and brightens the flavor.

MAKES 4 TO 6 SERVINGS

CAKE

1 cup (125 g) all-purpose flour

1 tsp baking soda

½ tsp salt

2 large eggs

Zest from 1 orange

¾ cup (144 g) granulated sugar

1 tbsp (14 g) room-temperature unsalted butter

4 tbsp (80 g) apricot jam

1 tsp distilled white vinegar

¾ cup (180 ml) milk

SAUCE

1 cup (240 ml) evaporated milk

8 tbsp (112 g) butter

¼ cup (36 g) brown sugar

1½ tsp (8 ml) vanilla extract

Preheat the oven to 350°F (177°C). Grease an 8- or 9-inch (20- or 23-cm) cake pan.

To make the cake, sift together the flour, baking soda and salt in a large bowl.

In another large bowl, whisk together the eggs, orange zest, granulated sugar, butter and jam. Add the vinegar and milk to the egg mixture and whisk to combine.

Gradually begin adding the flour to the egg mixture. Fold the two together until they are incorporated.

Pour the batter into the cake pan and bake for 25 minutes. The cake is ready when a toothpick inserted into the center comes out clean.

While the cake is baking, make the sauce. Heat the evaporated milk, butter, brown sugar and vanilla in a small pot over medium heat. Once the sugar has dissolved and the butter has melted, remove the pot from the heat. Stir the sauce.

Remove the cake from the oven and allow it to cool for 5 minutes. Poke small holes into the top of the cake using a toothpick or wooden skewer. Pour the sauce all over the cake.

Serve the malva pudding immediately or keep it chilled in the fridge until you are ready to serve.

STOCKING YOUR PANTRY FOR AFRICAN COOKING

African cooking can seem intimidating, especially if you don't know what ingredients to look or shop for. I've compiled this list of key ingredients that I use in most of the recipes in this book so that you can have a guide as to what you will need.

Most major grocery stores have an international aisle where you will be able to find some of the ingredients I mention here. Another one of my favorite places to get African ingredients is at Asian markets or, if you have these in your area, international farmer's markets. My first choice is always an African market—but if you lack these options, online shopping is another great resource.

These ingredients will be the building blocks to a lot of the recipes in this book, and keeping your pantry stocked with them means that you get to whip up delicious African meals whenever you feel like it.

AFRICAN BIRD'S EYE CHILE

One of the hottest peppers known to man, African bird's eye chiles are used in African cooking a lot! They are in just about every recipe, and they're used to give heat to chicken, meat, soups, stews and so on. Finding this chile in the United States can be tricky. You can try international farmer's markets; otherwise, habanero chiles are an excellent replacement.

AFRICAN NUTMEG (EHURU)

Fragrant and aromatic African nutmeg (ehuru) comes from the calabash nutmeg tree in West Africa and is often used to flavor soups, stews, cakes and desserts. The taste is very similar to nutmeg. You can find ehuru online.

ALL-PURPOSE FLOUR

Most of my breads, flatbreads, cakes and desserts are made with all-purpose flour, so you always want to keep a bag of flour handy.

ALL-PURPOSE SEASONING

All-purpose seasoning is a great way to add extra flavor to sauces, soups, stews—just about anything you are cooking. You can find it at most supermarkets.

BITTER LEAF

This is a widely used plant in Nigerian and West African cooking. Most vegetable soups will call for an addition of bitter leaf. Just like the name suggests, it is pretty bitter—but the flavor tends to mellow out when it's cooked. It's also a plant that is very medicinal and is used to treat a wide range of health conditions. Bitter leaf can be found at African markets or online.

BLACK-EYED PEAS, CHICKPEAS AND LENTILS

Black-eyed peas, chickpeas and lentils are very popular ingredients in Africa. They are usually seasoned heavily with spices common to each region. Usually, they will be paired with rice or stews or soups. All of these can be found at your local supermarket.

BOUILLON CUBES

Bouillon cubes are a great way to impart flavor into whatever you're cooking. A lot of African cooking involves using bouillon cubes as a flavoring agent. These are available at major supermarkets and any flavor will do.

CHUTNEY

Spicy condiments made of fruits and/or vegetables, chutneys are used in North and East African cooking as bases for soups and stews as well as condiments. The most popular variety is mango chutney, but the choice really depends on what you are making. You can find chutneys in the international aisle at your local supermarket or any Asian or Indian market.

COCONUT MILK

Canned coconut milk is commonly used in African cooking. Because of its richness and creaminess, it's often used to thicken soups and curries. It's also a great way to mellow out the large amount of spices and high level of heat found in African cooking.

CUMIN

Ground cumin is very prevalent in North and East African recipes. It's another flavor base that seasons meats, stews and vegetables. Find it at your local supermarket.

CURRY POWDER

A blend of coriander, turmeric, cumin, fenugreek and chiles, curry powder is added to soups and stews and serves as an aromatic base. You can use any curry powder you like and can easily find some at your local supermarket.

EGUSI MELON SEEDS

Egusi are fat- and protein-rich seeds from melon plants in Western Africa. The seeds are dried, ground and used to make Egusi Soup (page 18) and as a flavoring and thickening agent in some soups and stews. You can buy the seeds whole and grind them yourself, or you can buy the powder. Egusi is available at African markets and online. I have sometimes seen the powder in Indian and Asian markets.

GRAM FLOUR

Gram flour is flour that is made from chickpeas. It's very popular in North and East African cuisines and is often used to make breads and as a coating in fried dishes. Gram flour can be found at your local supermarket, international market or online.

GROUND CRAYFISH

Ground crayfish is used to flavor so many dishes in West African cooking. It adds a very traditional and earthy flavor and is a key ingredient in most soups and stews. You can find the powder at most African markets and online. Alternatively, you can find dried crayfish and grind them yourself.

GROUNDNUT OIL

Groundnut oil is a mild-tasting vegetable oil made from peanuts. This oil is commonly used to fry stews and meat. Most international farmer's markets carry it.

HEINZ BAKED BEANS

Heinz baked beans are very popular in Nigeria. They are used in the Nigerian Salad (page 58); in addition, people love to have them with their breakfast. Think of a "proper" English breakfast. These beans are less sweet than canned baked beans in the United States. These can be found in international markets or online.

HEINZ SALAD CREAM

Heinz Salad Cream is essential in making the Nigerian Salad (page 58). It's a creamy condiment that's been emulsified with oil and egg yolk, and it also has vinegar in it. It can be found at international markets or online.

JAGGERY

Jaggery is cane sugar that is concentrated from cane juice without the separation of the molasses and crystals, resulting in a golden-brown to dark-brown color. It is often used in African cooking to sweeten desserts. It can be found in Indian and Asian markets as well as online.

NIGERIAN RED PEPPER

Nigerian red pepper is the hotter and spicier version of cayenne pepper. It's got a lot of heat and is commonly used to add heat to soups and stews in West African cooking. You can get Nigerian red pepper at any African market or online.

PALM OIL

Palm oil is a vegetable oil derived from the fruit of the oil palms in Western Africa. Red in color, palm oil is often used to flavor soups and stews. You can also use it with boiled yam and plantains. Palm oil can be found at African and Asian markets.

PEPPER SOUP SPICE MIX

Pepper soup spice mix is a blend of African nutmeg, negro pepper (uda seeds) and alligator pepper that gives pepper soup that rich, spicy flavor. If you have access to these ingredients, you can blend them together and make the spice mix yourself. Otherwise, pepper soup spice mix can be found online and at African markets.

PLANTAINS

Plantains are very popular in African cooking. Whether they are fried, boiled, baked or broiled, having these in your pantry to eat with rice and stews is essential. You can get plantains in the produce aisle of most supermarkets.

RICE

A staple ingredient in African cooking, the most common varieties of rice used are parboiled, jasmine, basmati and long-grain. These can be found at most major supermarkets.

SWALLOW

Swallow refers to the starches used to "swallow" and accompany soups in Western Africa. These include but are not limited to Fufu (page 49) and Banku (page 50). The most popular swallow is fufu, which is made from powdered yam. Most swallows can be found at African markets or online.

TATASHE

Red bell peppers are a very common ingredient in African cooking. But unlike normal bell peppers, tatashe are red in color and have an elongated shape, like Romano peppers. You can get these at your local supermarket.

TEFF FLOUR

Teff flour comes from a gluten-free grain in Eastern Africa and is essential in East African cooking. It is used to make Injera (page 99), a national dish of Ethiopia. It can be found in African markets, international markets and online.

TOMATOES

Another popular ingredient in African cooking, tomatoes are blended into most sauces, soups and stews.

TOMATO PASTE

Because fresh tomatoes are used so often, tomato paste is used in accompaniment to enhance and bring out the tomato flavor.

TURMERIC

This spice is very common in most North and South African recipes. It has a distinct yellow color and is pungent and earthy in taste. It is used mostly in savory dishes. You can find turmeric at most local supermarkets.

YAM

Yam is another starch that is a very popular accompaniment to most African soups and stews. The most common way it is eaten is boiled or fried. It's also pounded to make fufu. African yam can be found at African markets or at any Asian or international market.

YAM POWDER

Yam powder comes from yam that has been pounded into a powder. It is what Fufu (page 49) is made from, which is commonly used as swallow to accompany soups. You can find yam powder in some Asian markets, international markets, all African markets and online.

ACKNOWLEDGMENTS

It has always been a dream of mine to write my own cookbook—and now that I've done it, I am still so amazed. It has been such an amazing and rewarding experience and so many people have contributed to my success along the way. It truly does take a village.

To my mum, I can never say thank you enough for the countless sacrifices you have made for me and our entire family. You are the hardest-working woman I've ever met and never complain about anything you go through. You are my inspiration and motivation, and you push me daily to become the best woman I can be. Ever since I started watching you cook in the kitchen, I've admired how full of love and life you are no matter what you do. This book is for you, and it really is yours because your teaching and guidance have ultimately led me to writing it in the first place. You make me so proud, and it's my joy to share your legacy with the world. I love you, and I may be biased, but you are the best mother anyone could ever have. I salute you.

To my sisters, Orezi and Oreva, you are my best friends! I can always call and talk to you about anything, and I always have your support. You both inspire and encourage me to go after my dreams and to not look back while doing so. You have truly seen how I've grown in the kitchen over the years, and as my first taste testers, you've always kept it real (even when I made that linguine that made Oreva sick). I love you guys.

To my dad, you have always pushed me to do what I love—and as I get older, I truly see how important that is. Thank you for always listening and for withholding judgment, even when I didn't always do what I was supposed to. You are a voice of reason and are a calm presence in my life. I love you.

To my extended family, our family is huge and I love it! I love family get-togethers and all of the delicious food we all bring to the table.

To Devin, my official taste tester, best friend and motivation during this entire process. Thank you for always being available and ready to help. From those late-night (and sometimes early morning) grocery runs to all-day photo shoots to my constantly asking, "How does this taste?" you have been such a vital part. Thank you for just being you.

To Lauren and the team at Page Street Publishing, thank you for believing in me to get this book done! Your belief in me made me achieve something that I thought I could never do.

To all my readers of Ev's Eats, foodie friends and blogging community, thank you for loving me and my recipes. Without you guys, none of this would be possible. Thank you for all the comments and feedback you have given me—it continues to inspire me every day. Thank you from the bottom of my heart. I love you all.

ABOUT THE AUTHOR

Evi Aki is the recipe developer, writer and photographer behind the blog Ev's Eats. As a lifelong foodie, she started her food blog in 2015 to introduce global flavors and spices that can be translated into easy recipes everyone can enjoy. With an emphasis on African and Caribbean recipes as well easy, family-friendly meals, Ev's Eats was created to share Evi's passion for good food, travel and photography.

When Evi isn't in the kitchen creating new recipes, she's still eating and can be found trying out restaurants in Los Angeles or traveling around the world, learning new cuisines and experiences, which she also shares on her blog.

Evi is a travel contributor to The Daily Meal and has various articles featured on the The Daily Meal's site. Her recipes and videos have been featured on numerous websites, including MSN.com, BuzzFeed, Brit + Co, Yahoo, Kontrol Magazine and Cowgirl Magazine.

INDEX